W. N. Hutchinson

Brigade Drill

As Established by Order in the Field Exercise and Evolutions of Infantry

W. N. Hutchinson

Brigade Drill

As Established by Order in the Field Exercise and Evolutions of Infantry

ISBN/EAN: 9783743411296

Manufactured in Europe, USA, Canada, Australia, Japa

Cover: Foto ©Andreas Hilbeck / pixelio.de

Manufactured and distributed by brebook publishing software (www.brebook.com)

W. N. Hutchinson

Brigade Drill

BRIGADE DRILL,

*As Established by Order in the Field Exercise
and Evolutions of Infantry, as revised in*

1861.

WITH

REMARKS AND REFERENCES.

BY

MAJOR-GENERAL W. N. HUTCHINSON,
COMMANDING WESTERN DISTRICT.

LONDON:
PARKER, SON, & BOURN, 445, WEST STRAND.
M DCCC LXII.

PREFACE.

At the suggestion of parties who found the little work I wrote on Brigade Drill of use, when the Field Exercise and Evolutions established in 1833 were in force, I have drawn up another Book on a similar plan ; but my task has been far easier. All is so plainly laid down in the present *Field Exercise* that I have had little more to do than to arrange in methodical order, and place in a tabular form, what has been therein very clearly expressed.

As in every Manœuvre of a Regiment it ought to be drilled as if holding a *designated* place in a Brigade, I think the tabular sheets* will be found serviceable to those who are merely studying Battalion Drill, for in all changes the position of Aides, Officers, and Coverers is fully detailed.

Government House,
Devonport,
June 23rd, 1860.

---

* Now altered according to the revised copy issued in February 1862.

Government House,
Devonport,
February 27th, 1862.

CONTENTS.

	PAGE
Division of Bodies of Troops	11
By whom, and how formed up	11
Distance of Battalions and Brigades from each other	12
Points of Formation	13
Dressing of Points	16
Commands	17
General Observations	18
A Brigade in Mass of Columns, at Close or Quarter Distance, wheeling into a Line of Columns	22
A Brigade in Line of Contiguous, Close, or Quarter Distance Columns, wheeling into Mass	26
A Brigade in Mass of Battalion Columns, at Close or Quarter Distance, deploying into Line of Contiguous Battalion Columns	30
A Brigade in Mass of Battalion Columns, at Close or Quarter Distance, deploying into Line of Contiguous Battalion Columns on a central Battalion	34
A Brigade in Line of Contiguous Battalion Columns, at Close or Quarter Distance, forming Mass upon any named Battalion	38
A Brigade in Line of Contiguous Battalion Columns, at Close or Quarter Distance, forming Mass upon any named Battalion	42
A Brigade in Line of Contiguous, Close, or Quarter Distance Columns, changing Front	46

CONTENTS.

	PAGE
A Brigade in Line of Contiguous, Close, or Quarter Distance Columns changing Front on a Central Battalion (the depth of Columns exceeding their breadth)	50
A Brigade advancing in Line or retiring in Line	54
A Brigade advancing or retiring in Line of Contiguous Columns	58
A Brigade advancing or retiring in Line of Quarter Distance Columns, at deploying Distance	62
A Brigade formed in Line of Double Columns, at deploying Distance, advancing or retiring	66
A Brigade in Line advancing in Open Columns from the flanks of Battalions, or in Double Column from the centre of Battalions	70
A Brigade retiring in Open Column of Companies, from the one flank of Battalions in rear of the other, or from both flanks of Battalions in rear of their centres	74
A Brigade advancing in Double Column of Companies from the centre, or retiring by Companies from both flanks in rear of the centre	78
The Brigade retiring in Double Column of Companies from both flanks in rear of its centre	82
A Brigade standing in Double Column of Companies forming Line to the Front (the whole Brigade in one Double Column)	86
A Brigade in Double Column of Companies forming Line to a flank	90
A Brigade (from Line) advancing in open Column of Companies from either flank, or retiring by Companies from one flank in rear of the other	94
A Brigade in Line changing Front on a named Company of a named Battalion	98

CONTENTS.

	PAGE
A Brigade in Line changing Front on a named Company of a named Battalion	102
A Brigade from Line changing Position on Detached Points	106
A Brigade from Line changing Position on Detached Points	110
A Brigade in Line of Contiguous Columns, at Close or Quarter Distance, deploying into Line	114
A Brigade in Mass of Battalion Columns opening out to deploying Distance on Detached Points, and deploying into Line	118
A Brigade advancing from a Line by the flank March of Fours	122
A Brigade from Line forming Square	126
Two Lines changing Front on the flank of the first Line	130
Two Lines changing Front upon a central Point of the first Line	134
Advances and Retreats	137
Echellons, Direct and Oblique	137
Inversions and Changes of Front	140
Movements to be Covered by Light Infantry	140
Reserves	141
Position of Artillery	141
Review of two or more Battalions	142
Formation in Columns	143
Marching past in Columns	145
,, ,, in Open Column	146
,, ,, in "Grand Divisions"	146
Advancing in Review Order	146
Order of March at Reviews	147
Official Memorandum,—Words of Command for a Volunteer Review, 1860	148
Copies of two District Orders	150, 152

BRIGADE DRILL.

Division of Bodies of Troops.

" GREAT bodies of troops are formed into one or more
" lines, and are divided into right and left wings, or into corps
" d'armée, each wing or corps d'armée is divided into divisions,
" each division into brigades, and each brigade is composed of
" two, three, or more battalions." (p. 446.)

By whom, and how formed up.

" When taking up an alignment for a large body of troops,
" the assistant adjutant-general of the base division will mark
" the point of appui, and the assistant quartermasters-general
" will mark the distant points for their respective divisions,
" the adjutant-general dressing them from the point of appui.
" When the troops approach the alignment, the brigade-majors
" will move up with their foot or mounted points to take up the
" ground for their respective brigades, under the superin-
" tendence of their assistant adjutants-general. The assistant
" quartermasters-general, when they are dressed, may be re-
" placed by mounted orderlies if it is considered more con-
" venient." (p. 450.)

" When a brigade-major is required to take up ground at a
" distance, for his brigade, and is not informed on which flank
" he will have to form, he may be obliged to take two or more
" majors of the brigade as well as the adjutants with him, in
" case he should be required to give the point of appui."
(p. 451.)

"It may also be necessary in some cases to send on mounted points to take up ground for a brigade in contiguous columns. In this case one major and one adjutant will usually be enough to mark the flanks of the brigade, and they will be relieved at once when the coverers and supernumeraries move up." (p. 451.)

"Any mounted officers who are not required to mark points should be sent back by the brigade-major to their battalions." (p. 451.)

Distance of Battalions and Brigades from each other.

"Battalions in line will be drawn up at the distance of six paces from each other. No increased distance should be allowed between brigades or divisions unless specially ordered." (p. 447.)

"Columns in line with intervals of six paces between them are called contiguous columns. This is the least distance at which columns should be formed. The intervals between columns in line may vary from six paces to deploying distance, according to circumstances and at the discretion of the commander." (p. 447.)

"*Formation of Open Column.*—When divisions or brigades are formed in open column of route or manœuvre, the distances between battalions must be equal to the breadth of the leading company of the column and six paces; thus, should the battalions wheel into line, the interval of six paces will be preserved between them." (p. 447.)

"*Mass of Columns.*—When a brigade is formed in mass of close or quarter distance columns, the intervals between battalions will be six paces." (p. 447.)

Points of Formation.

" The field officers and adjutant, when with the battalion,
" are at all times to be mounted, in order to take up ground,
" dress points and pivots, correct mistakes, and circulate orders.
" They should always know the number of files in the battalion
" and in its companies, and be able to take up the distance
" required for the whole or any part of its front. This may be
" done by counting the strides of their horses when cantering;
" but the eye will be found the most convenient and accurate
" guide in judging distances. The majors and adjutant, when
" they are not marking points, must afford every assistance to
" the commanding officer during a manœuvre, and move to
" their places when it is done." (p. 219.)

" When only one major is present the senior captain should,
" if practicable, be mounted. When this cannot be done, the
" adjutant will take the place of the junior major; if only one
" mounted officer is present, besides the commanding officer, he
" must be prepared to dress the coverers from either flank or to
" give distant points, as may be required; the commander must
" also assist in dressing the coverers, and the serjeant-major
" will be available for that duty so far as it can be performed
" on foot." (p. 219.)

" *Giving Points.*—When mounted officers give points, they
" must place their horses at right angles with the alignment,
" facing towards it, and in deploying into or forming line the
" horses' heads will be dressed at arm's length from the align-
" ment. The bodies of the dismounted points will be dressed
" in the same line as the horses' heads." (pp. 219, 220.)

" When a mounted officer accompanying a movement leads
" a column or preserves deploying distance from it, while it is
" on the march, he will keep his own face in line with the leading
" rank of the column. In brigade movements, mounted officers

" giving points must not fall back to their posts until dismissed
" by signal from the brigade-major." (p. 451.)

" When forming or deploying into a line of contiguous
" columns, the coverers and supernumerary serjeants of the
" leading companies of battalions will mark the alignment,
" giving their points at arm's length in front of the line on
" which the companies are to dress, as directed in Part IV.,
" General Principle V. The coverers will mark the outer flanks
" of the leading companies of their respective battalions; the
" supernumerary serjeants of the leading company of the
" battalion of formation will mark the point of appui; the
" supernumerary serjeants of the leading companies of the
" remaining battalions will mark the inner flanks of their re-
" spective companies, each preserving the interval of six paces
" from the outer flank of the battalion next to him towards the
" point of appui." (p. 448.)

" In wheeling from mass into line of columns, the pivot
" men and the coverers of the leading companies of battalions,
" placed as described in Part IV., Section 16, will be a suffi-
" cient guide to preserve the alignment." (p. 448.)

" In the above formations the brigade-major will, as usual,
" dress the points and pivots from the point of appui." (p. 448.)

" In the formation of a mass of columns, the leaders of
" companies will preserve the line of covering, the brigade-
" major correcting their covering from the point of appui.
" When the formation is on a central or rear battalion or com-
" pany of the mass, the leaders in front of the point of appui
" will face about to cover, and will come to the front again on
" the brigade-major's word *Steady*, which may be given to each
" battalion in succession. The men should not be ordered to
" dress until the leaders of companies have completed their
" covering." (p. 448.)

" In all deployments or formations into line, or into line of
" columns at deploying distance, the general alignment will be

" preserved by mounted officers. The brigade point of appui
" will be marked by a major of the battalion of formation.
" When the formation is on the right flank of the base battalion,
" the senior major will mark the point of appui, when on the
" left flank, the junior major will mark that point; in both
" cases the adjutant will mark the distant flank. When the
" formation is on the centre, or on a central company of the
" base battalion, the senior major will mark the point of appui,
" the junior major the left flank, and the adjutant the right
" flank; in each case the adjutants of the remaining battalions
" of the brigade will mark the outer flanks of their respective
" corps. No mounted points will be required on their inner
" flanks, the supernumerary serjeant of the company on that
" flank of each battalion which is nearest to the base battalion,
" preserving the usual interval of six paces from the outer
" flank of the battalion next to him towards the point of appui."
(pp. 448, 449.)

" When a battalion, not being the battalion of formation,
" moves up, either in single or double column, to a central point
" of the alignment on which it is required to deploy or form
" line, as represented by the centre battalion in Plate LX., the
" central base points ($h, h, h,$) of the battalion will be dressed
" by the major (l), assisted by the serjeant-major (m), on the
" points ($e, d,$ or $n, n, n,$) of the battalion of formation; but
" the remaining battalion points ($o, o, o,$) will cover on the
" centre of their own battalion, as usual. The adjutant (f)
" will mark the outward flank, dressing on the brigade point
" of appui, but no other mounted point will be necessary."
(p. 449.)

" When battalions form line or deploy in succession, they
" will complete their formation or deployment, each battalion
" in succession preserving the interval of six paces from the
" outer flank of the previously formed battalion, although the
" adjutants may not have taken correct distance; the majors

" will, however, dress all the coverers from adjutant to adjutant,
" in the same manner as a captain in the deployment of a
" battalion dresses all the men from coverer to coverer, whether
" they belong to his company or not. When battalions deploy
" simultaneously, and the space they have to occupy is con-
" sequently limited, as would be the case were a line of battalion
" columns formed at deploying distance required to deploy,
" they must not go beyond their outward points; if the
" distances are not sufficient, the companies or parts of com-
" panies for which there is no room must be formed in rear of
" the line, where they will be directed to order arms and stand
" at ease until space is made for them by order of the general
" commanding the troops." (pp. 449, 450.)

" Field movements and firings are to be performed with
" fixed bayonets, except by rifle corps and by other troops when
" acting as light infantry. See Part II., General Principles,
" XIX., Rule 9." (p. 221.)

Dressing of Points.

" The dressing of points in an alignment will be much
" facilitated by selecting some clearly defined distant point,
" such as a house or a windmill, in its prolongation, which may
" be used by the assistant adjutants-general or brigade-majors
" as the outer point on which they may dress their intermediate
" points." (p. 451.)

" To enable intermediate points to take up their covering
" correctly in an alignment, a second point will occasionally be
" required outside of the point of appui, as a guide to the
" distant points; this point must be correctly dressed on the
" prolongation of the alignment. By means of successive
" points covering on this base, a formation may be prolonged in
" a straight line, to any extent." (p. 220.)

"As a general rule, the major nearest to the point of "formation will dress the coverers or pivots. The senior "major will dress the coverers or pivots when the formation "is on the centre of the battalion." (pp. 220, 221.)

Commands.

"Cautions given by the general to a brigade or division "in line, in line of columns at deploying distance, or in "echellon, will be passed by all the mounted officers; but when "a caution is given to a brigade or division in line of con- "tiguous columns, or in mass, it will be repeated only by the "commanders of battalions. In order that words of com- "mand may be circulated with precision and rapidity, the "eye and attention of each battalion leader must be con- "stantly directed to the commanding general, or to the regu- "lating battalion when he cannot be heard. Officers must "take care properly to understand an order before passing "it." (pp. 451, 452.)

"On the caution from the general of the division or "brigade all interior movements of battalions will be made, "so that the whole may be ready to step off at the executive "command, which each battalion, on all occasions, will re- "ceive from its own leader." (p. 452.)

"To enable the commanders of battalions to give their "executive words of command simultaneously, the general "should give some signal by gesture, such as holding up his "sword, or by bugle sound, on which the commanders will "give their executive words; or he may order the commanders "to take time from the battalion of direction." (p. 452.)

"The cautions of the general commanding the division "or brigade must be expressed in terms which cannot be mis-

B

" taken by the soldiers for battalion words of command."
(p. 452.)

" When the progress of an order from battalion to
" battalion is interrupted by any cause, such as wind or the
" noise of fire-arms, the commanders will conform as quickly
" as possible to the movement they see executed by the bat-
" talion of direction." (p. 452.)

" Generals will also make use of their staff officers to
" convey orders to distant battalions; the advance or halt
" may be communicated to large bodies of troops by sound
" of bugle when considered necessary." (p. 452.)

The major who is on the outer flank of a battalion should repeat the general's caution until it is taken up by the next battalion.

General Observations.

There is great uniformity throughout the whole drill. What are changes of position on a central point but throwing forward one part of the moved body, and backward the other?

A man facing to the right throws "forward the left" (shoulder), and "backward the right." A company wheeling on its centre to the right, throws "forward the left" (sub-division), and "backward the right."

A battalion in line changing on its centre to the right, throws "forward the left" (wing), and "backward the right." A brigade in line changing its direction to the right on a central battalion, throws "forward the left" (the battalions on its left), and "backward the right" (the battalions on the right).

When the change is on the centre, it is manifest that if one flank be thrown forward, the other flank must be thrown back; therefore, that a commander may indifferently order one wing to be thrown forward, or the other wing to be thrown backward, for, in either case, the result will be the same.

In the same way that when at company's drill the instructor states whether the battalion is supposed to be right or left in front (IX. p. 62, and Part II. p. 218),—so at battalion drill when any distance column is advancing or retiring its commander should state (for guidance of mounted points) whether it is to be considered the directing battalion, or should be regulated by a battalion on its right or left—also whether the supposed brigade is moving in line of contiguous columns, or in line of columns at deploying distance,* &c.

" A battalion may be considered to hold in a brigade or
" line the relative situation of a company in a battalion, and
" it will be found that the principles laid down in Part IV.
" for the movements of the battalion, will apply in a great
" measure to the movements of a brigade." (No. 1, p. 446.)

Suppose that a brigade (or battalion), standing in line, has to form mass (or column) right in front on any central battalion (or company), the battalions (or companies) standing on the right of the named battalion (or company) lead (disengage) to the front, and then to the left. The battalions (or companies) standing on the left of the named battalion (or company) lead (disengage) to the rear, and then to the right.

Deploying a mass of battalions on any named battalion is the same as deploying a column (a mass) of companies on any named company. The battalions which are to stand on the right of the line move to the right; those which are to stand on the left of the line move to the left; and further, supposing all right in front, it would be the troops (both in

* At the end of this book a copy will be found of a district order issued on that subject.

brigade and battalion drill) standing in front of the body " of formation," who would move to the right; those standing in its rear to the left. Moreover, the central company of a battalion, on its front being cleared, comes up to the front of the line at the double, having previously (on the caution) given base points for the battalion; so does the central battalion of a brigade move up to the line, on its front being clear, having previously (on the caution) given base points for the brigade.

In all changes Officers commanding battalions will have to pay attention that their points move out in sufficient time. Some commanders make a practice of giving the word " *Base Points*," or " *Out Base*," for the supernumerary and covering serjeant, when their battalions get within twenty paces of a new alignment.

When nothing is said to the contrary, it is supposed in the following tabular sheets that the brigade consists of four battalions, (numbered 1, 2, 3, 4, from right to left,) each of six companies—that there is no inversion—that columns are right in front, and that there is a lieutenant-colonel and two majors with each battalion.

The approximate position during all movements of the mounted officers is named, but it must be borne in mind that " the majors and adjutant when they are not marking points " must afford every assistance to the commanding officer " during a manœuvre, and move to their places when it is " done." (IV. p. 219.)

In contiguous quarter distance columns each band, formed in two ranks, will be in rear of its column,—but when the columns are in mass, their bands, formed in several ranks, will be on their respective reverse flanks. (No. 2, p. 250.)

The manœuvres of divisions or larger bodies of troops " are performed simply by a succession of Brigade move-" ments." (See 22, p. 493.)

No. I.

Sec. 1, p. 459.

A Brigade in Mass of Columns, at Close or Quarter Distance, wheeling into a Line of Columns.

Sec. 1, p. 459. A Brigade in Mass of Columns, at Close

Brigadier.	Commanders of Battalions.	Coverers and Supernumerary Serjeants.
The Brigade will wheel into Line of Contiguous Columns. (Suppose right of Brigade in front.) Signal or bugle.	All repeat, "The Brigade will wheel into Line of Contiguous Columns." All, "No. —, Left wheel." Lieutenants move up to lead on reverse flank. All, "Quick March." All, "Halt," each when his leading Company is completing its wheel. Lieutenants resume their places, and no one stirs unless the word "Dress" is given, when the men take up their dressing by the left (the pivot flank) (3).	Each Covering Serjeant of a leading Company marks where outer flank of his column will rest on completion of wheel, aligning with the pivot man who had faced to the left on caution. He raises his left arm (1). No Supernumeraries move out.

REMARKS.——The wheel is usually to the pivot flank. If required, the wheel could be made at the double (6). If the wheel is to the reverse flank, the caution would be given that the wheel would be to the right, which would invert the Brigade. Prior to such wheel the columns would in all probability have been previously dressed "By the right," in the manner described in the remarks, page 26.

After the Battalions are wheeled into line, it is obvious that they will stand six paces apart, plus the number of paces by which the breadth of each column is exceeded by the depth of the column which stood in its immediate front when in mass.

Part of Field Exercise Book authorizing.——(1) p. 262.   (2) p. 263,

Brigade Major.	Post of Mounted Regimental Officers.	
	During Movement.	Movement completed.
Goes to rear of rear Battalion to dress the line of pivots and coverers from the flank of the rear Battalion of the column.	Lieutenant-Colonel (2) near pivot. Senior Major (2) reverse flank of leading Company to regulate its pace. Junior Major (2) in rear of reverse flank to see that outer files retain their relative positions. Adjutant near centre of reverse flank to see that Companies close up to leading files (2).	Lieutenant-Colonel (4) on pivot flank of leading Company. Senior Major (4) two paces from reverse flank of centre of right wing. Junior Major (4) two paces from reverse flank of centre of left wing. Adjutant (4) two paces from reverse flank of right centre Company.

After wheeling into line of contiguous columns, the Battalions may be ordered to close to six paces interval on any Battalion which then becomes the Battalion of formation; and the pivot flank of that Battalion becomes the point of appui. The Supernumerary Serjeant and Coverer of its leading Company instantly give base points. The base points of the other Battalions cover on them.

The point of appui is the pivot man of the leading Company of the rear Battalion.

Each Band in two ranks moves to rear of its column (5).

The Drummers, Fifers, Buglers, and Pioneers, in the supernumerary rank of their respective Companies (4).

Plate XXVII.   (3) p. 261.   (4) pp. 250, 225.   (5) p. 250.   (6) p. 264.

No. II.

Sec. 2, p. 459.

A Brigade in Line of Contiguous, Close, or Quarter Distance Columns, wheeling into Mass.

Brigadier.	Commanders of Battalions.	Coverers and Supernumerary Serjeants.
The Brigade will (say) right wheel into mass. Signal or Bugle.	All, "*The Brigade will Right wheel into Mass.*" All, " *No. —, Right wheel.*" All, " *Quick (or double) March.*" "*Halt,*" each when his leading Company is completing its wheel. No man stirs unless the word "*Dress*" is given, when the men take up their dressing by the left, the pivot* flank (1). * In Wheeling, the "standing flank" is called the pivot flank (5), but after the completion of the wheel it is only accidentally that it can be the pivot flank.	The Covering Serjeant of every leading Company runs out to mark where the outward flank of his column will rest when the wheel is completed. Every pivot man — viz. the right hand man of front rank of leading Company—faces, his rear rank man uncovers (1).

REMARKS.——Where the depth of each Battalion, as is usually the case, exceeds its breadth of front, Battalions must be opened out to a distance sufficient to admit of the wheel, allowing also for the six paces interval. This is generally done,—and by the side step when the Brigade is working singly,—but when it forms part of a division it may be necessary to bring the quarter distance columns into close columns (to give space) prior to wheeling into mass. But close column formations must not be adopted in the general evolutions of a Brigade (3).

Should it be intended to move the column as soon as it is in mass, it will not

Part of Field Exercise Book authorizing.——(1) p. 262.   (2) p. 263, Plate

Close, or Quarter Distance Columns, wheeling into Mass. 27

Brigade Major.	Post of Mounted Regimental Officers.	
	During Movement.	Movement completed.
After the completion of the wheel, should dressing of pivots be ordered, the Brigade Major from the front and left sees that the Captains cover. He will be assisted by a Field Officer.	Lieutenant-Colonel on right near pivot (2). Senior Major (2) reverse flank (left) of the leading Company. Junior Major (2) in rear of reverse flank (left), seeing that outer files (the Captains) retain their covering. Adjutant near centre of proper reverse flank, to see that Companies close up to leading files (2).	Lieutenant-Colonel on pivot flank of leading Company (4). Senior Major two paces from reverse flank of centre of right wing (4). Junior Major two paces from reverse flank of centre of left wing (4). Adjutant two paces from reverse flank of right centre Company (4).

be necessary to dress the pivots. The Captains will gain their covering on the march. But if it be necessary to dress the pivots correctly, the Captains will be covered from the front by the Brigade Major, assisted by the Commanders of Battalions or the Majors, the men standing fast. When the Captains are correctly covered, on the word "*Dress*" from the Battalion Commanders, the men will close to, and dress upon their Captains. Had the wheel been to the left, this dressing could not have been necessary,—the mass would have been left in front, —but each Battalion still right in front,—and the line of pivots would have been preserved.

XXVII. (3) VII. p. 248.   (4) pp. 250, 225.   (5) Sec. 27, p. 34.

No. III.

Sec. 3, p. 460.

A Brigade in Mass of Battalion Columns, at Close or Quarter Distance, deploying into Line of Contiguous Battalion Columns.

Sec. 3, p. 460. A Brigade in Mass of Battalion Columns Contiguous Battalion Columns

Brigadier.	Commanders of Battalions.	Coverers and Supernumerary Serjeants.
The Brigade will deploy into line of contiguous columns on the leading Battalion. (Suppose right of Brigade in front.) Bugle or signal.	All, "*The Brigade will deploy into Line of Contiguous Columns on the leading Battalion.*" All (except leading Battalion), "*Form Fours Left,*" "*By the Right.*" All, "*Quick March.*" Commander of No. 2, when six paces beyond No. 1, "*Front Turn,*" "*By the Right,*" Lieutenants leading, "*Halt.*"—"*Dress,*" if necessary. Commander of No. 3, on No. 2 receiving word, "*Front turn,*" "*Right Half turn,*" "*Front turn,*" "*By the Right,*" Lieutenants move up, "*Halt.*" —"*Dress,*" if necessary. Commander of No. 4, ditto, ditto.	Supernumerary Serjeant and Coverer of front Company of named Battalion facing to the right give base points at arm's length from front of their column. The Supernumerary marks the point of appui, the Coverer, the distance of his Company. Coverer and Supernumerary Serjeant of each leading Company of other Battalions, when within twenty paces of the alignment, run up and cover on the base points; Supernumerary Serjeants answerable for six paces, Coverers for distance of their respective Companies (1).

REMARKS.——As line is formed on a right Battalion, it is clear that the other Battalions must come into position by the right, and that all dressing of front Companies must be from the right, but the Captains are dressed from the left. Many good drills never allow the men to dress until the Captains have received the word, "Steady" (8). The Brigade point of appui is on the right, in the

Part of Field Exercise Book authorizing.——(1) No. 3, p. 448. (2) p. 250. (7) p. 315.

at Close or Quarter Distance, deploying into Line of on leading Battalion.

Brigade Major.	Post of Mounted Regimental Officers.	
	During Movement.	Movement completed.
From the right dresses the base foot points of the front Battalion (the Battalion of formation) and, successively, the Supernumeraries and Coverers of the other Battalions on them. The Supernumerary Serjeant of front Company of leading Battalion marks point of appui (1).	The Lieutenant-Colonel of No. 1 stands fast on left (3). The Lieutenant-Colonels of Nos. 2, 3, 4, are in rear near the inner (the right flank), watching when to change direction of their respective Battalions. Senior Majors see that Lieutenants of leading Companies lead correctly, and when on the alignment dress their respective leading Companies from the right (4). Junior Majors (6) look to covering of Lieutenants from the rear (2), and see that they retain their relative positions, such positions that the Captains will be found to cover when the column is halted (5). Adjutants near centre of right flanks — the proper reverse flank (3).	Lieutenant-Colonels on pivot flank (the left) of their several leading Companies, aligning with them (3). Senior Majors two paces from reverse flank, near centre of their several right wings (3). Junior Majors two paces from reverse flank, near centre of their respective left wings (3). Adjutants two paces from reverse flank of their right centre Companies (3).

same way that a Battalion point of appui is on the right when it deploys on a front Company (7).

The Lieutenant of each front Company of a Battalion marching up, leads on his Supernumerary Serjeant.

(3) pp. 225, 250. (4) p. 220. (5) p. 461. (6) note, p. 63, this book.
(8) No. 4, p. 448.

No. IV.

Sec. 3, p. 460.

'igade in Mass of Battalion Columns, at Close or Quarter Distance, deploying into Line of Contiguous Battalion Columns on a Central Battalion.

34 Sec. 3, p. 460. *A Brigade in Mass of Battalion Columns, tiguous Battalion Columns*

Brigadier.	Commanders of Battalions.	Coverers and Supernumerary Serjeants.
The Brigade will deploy into line of contiguous columns on (say) No. 2 Battalion. (Suppose right of Brigade in front.)	All repeat, "*The Brigade will deploy into line of Contiguous Columns on No. 2 Battalion.*" Commander of No. 2, "*No. 2 will advance*," "*By the Left*" (2). Commander of No. 1, "*Form Fours Right*," "*By the Left*" (when Lieutenants lead) (1). Commanders of Nos. 3 and 4, "*Form Fours Left*," "*By the Right.*"	Supernumerary Serjeant and Coverer of front Company of No. 2 run out and give the base points at arm's length from the front of the mass facing inwards, the former marking the point of appui (2). Supernumerary and Coverer of front Company of other Battalions run out when twenty paces from alignment to cover on base points. All face to the
Bugle or signal.	All (excepting Commander of No. 2), "*Quick March.*" No. 2, when front is clear, "*By the Left*," "*Double March.*"(5)"*Halt.*" No. 1, when six paces beyond No. 2, "*Halt, Front.*" No. 3, when six paces beyond No. 2, "*Front turn*," "*By the Right*," Lieutenants move up, "*Halt.*" "*Dress*," if necessary, when front as well as other Companies dress by the left. No. 4, when clear of No. 3, "*Right half turn.*" When six paces beyond No. 3, "*Front turn*," "*By the Right*," Lieutenants move up, &c.	left towards point of appui. The Supernumeraries mark the inner flank (the six paces), the Coverers, Company's distance (8).

REMARKS.——Line being formed on a central Battalion, it is evident that Battalions on the right must come into the alignment by the left—led by their Captains, and Battalions on the left by the right—led by their Lieutenants (6).

Part of Field Exercise Book authorizing.——(1) No. 8, p. 66.   (2) Plate LVI.
(7) note, p. 63, this book.

at Close or Quarter Distance, deploying into Line of Con- on a Central Battalion.

Brigade Major.	Post of Mounted Regimental Officers.	
	During Movement.	Movement completed.
From the left of No. 1 places base points of No. 2 (the Supernumerary Serjeant marking point of appui), and on them dresses the other points.	The Lieutenant-Colonels of Nos. 2 and 1 are on the left, directing the movement of their respective Battalions (3). Lieutenant-Colonels of Nos. 3 and 4 during the flank movement on the right — during the advance, near the rear on inner flank. Senior Majors see that their columns are led properly—when in line dress their respective leading Companies from flank nearest to point of appui. Junior Majors (7) of Nos. 2, 3, and 4 look to the covering of leaders of Companies (whether Captains or Lieutenants) from the rear, and see that Lieutenants preserve their relative positions (4). Each Adjutant near centre of proper reverse flank (3).	Each Lieutenant-Colonel on the left (pivot flank) of his leading Company (3), aligning with it. Each Senior Major two paces from reverse flank, near centre of his right wing (3). Each Junior Major two paces from reverse flank, near centre of his left wing (3). Each Adjutant two paces from reverse flank of right centre Company (3).

Of course No. 1 is an exception. During the advance the leader of each leading Company leads on his Supernumerary Serjeant.

(3) pp. 225, 250.   (4) p. 250.   (5) p. 491.   (6) p. 461.
(8) No. 3, p. 448.

No. V.

Sec. 4, p. 462.

A Brigade in Line of Contiguous Battalion Columns, at Close or Quarter Distance, forming Mass upon any named Battalion.

Sec. 4, p. 462. *A Brigade in Line of Contiguous forming Mass upon*

Brigadier.	Commander of Battalions.	Coverers and Supernumerary Serjeants.
Form Mass in rear of right Battalion. Signal or bugle.	All, "*Form Mass in Rear of Right Battalion.*" All, (except Commander of No. 1, which Battalion stands fast,) "*Right about Face.*" "*By the Left.*"* Lieutenants move up (1). "*Quick March.*" Lieutenants lead (1). Commander of No. 2, as soon as his proper front is six paces in rear of No. 1, "*Form Fours Left.*" Commanders of Nos. 3 and 4, when clear of column on their left, "*Left half turn,*" &c. All in succession, (except Commander of No.1,) "*Halt,*" "*Front,*" "*Dress.*" * "By the Left," see remarks.	Do not move out.

REMARKS.—— After the Battalions are faced about, the Battalion of formation stands on their left, therefore they must march into position "*By the Left,*" (the proper right.) led by the Lieutenants (1).

" The Captain of the leading Company of each Battalion which forms in rear " of another will be responsible for the six paces distance from such other Batta-" lion; and the Captain of the rear Company of each Battalion which forms in " front of another, will be responsible for that distance.

" The order in which the Battalions of a Brigade are arranged in mass does

Part of Field Exercise Book authorizing.——(1) p. 461.

Battalion Columns, at Close or Quarter Distance, any named Battalion.

Brigade Major.	Post of Mounted Regimental Officers.	
	During Movement.	Movement completed.
From the front of No. 1, assisted by the Commander or Senior Major, attends to covering of Captains.	Lieutenant-Colonels of 2, 3, and 4 on proper left flank near the proper front, watching to make the flank move in fours as soon as the proper front of their respective Battalions gets six paces in rear of Battalion just formed in mass. Senior Majors (2) from proper front of their respective Battalions, see that Lieutenants retain their relative positions (3)—such positions that Captains will be found to cover when the Battalion is halted and fronted (1). Junior Majors (2) near centre of left wings on proper reverse flank. Adjutants (2) near centre of Battalions on proper reverse flank.	Each Lieutenant-Colonel (2) on the left — the pivot flank, aligning with leading Company. Each Senior Major (2) two paces from reverse flank of centre of right wing. Each Junior Major (2) the same on centre of left wing. Each Adjutant (2) two paces from reverse flank of right centre Company.

" not in any way affect their pivot flanks ; thus, although the Battalion which
" stood on the left of the Brigade when in line of contiguous columns, may be
" formed in front of the mass, if each Battalion is right in front the left will be
" the pivot flank of the whole mass.

" When a line of contiguous columns thus forms mass, the Battalions need
" only move perpendicularly, until clear of the columns on the right or left, when
" each Commander will cut off the right angle by the diagonal march."

(2) pp. 225, 250.   (3) note, p. 63, this book.

No. VI.

Sec. 4, p. 462.

A Brigade in Line of Contiguous Battalion Columns, at Close or Quarter Distance, forming Mass upon any named Battalion.

Sec. 4, p. 462. A Brigade in Line of Contiguous forming Mass upon

Brigadier.	Commanders of Battalions.	Coverers and Supernumerary Serjeants.
Form mass in front of the right Battalion.	All, " *Form Mass in Front of the Right Battalion.*" All, (except Commander of No. 1, which Battalion stands fast,) No. — " *Will advance*," " *By the Right* " (4). Lieutenants move up (1).	Do not move out.
Bugle or signal.	All, (except No. 1,) " *Quick March.*" Lieutenants leading (1). No. 2, " *Form Fours Right.*" Nos. 3 and 4, when clear of column on their right, " *Right half turn*," &c. All, (except No. 1,) " *Halt, Front, Dress.*" No. 2, " *Halt, Front.*" Nos. 3 and 4 in succession, " *Halt, Front, Dress.*"	

REMARKS.——Forming mass on a central Battalion, the Brigadier's word of command would be, " *Form Mass Right (or Left) in Front on the — Battalion.*"

" The Captain of the leading Company of each Battalion which forms in rear " of another will be responsible for the six paces distance from such other Bat-" talion; and the Captain of the rear Company of each Battalion which forms in " front of another, will be responsible for that distance.

" The order in which the Battalions of a brigade are arranged in mass does " not in any way affect their pivot flanks; thus, although the Battalion which

Part of Field Exercise Book authorizing.——(1) p. 461.   (2) p. 448, No. 4.

Battalion Columns, at Close or Quarter Distance, any named Battalion. 43

Brigade Major.	Post of Mounted Regimental Officers.	
	During Movement.	Movement completed.
From the rear of the mass, assisted by the Lieutenant-Colonels or Majors, attends to covering of Captains. They come to the front on his word "Steady," which he would act judiciously in giving to Battalions in succession (2).	Lieutenant-Colonels of Nos. 2, 3, and 4 on left flank near the rear, watching to make the flank march in fours as the rear of their respective Battalions gains six paces to the front of the leading Company of the Battalion in rear of it in mass. Senior Majors on the right flank see that their several Battalions are led correctly. Junior Majors (5) from the rear of their Battalions look to covering of Officers on the march (4), and on "Halt," assist Brigade Major in the covering of the Captains. Adjutants near centre of Battalions on reverse flank (4).	Lieutenant-Colonel (3) on the left, the pivot flank of leading Company aligning with it. Senior Major (3) two paces on reverse flank of centre of right wing. Junior Major (3) the same centre of left wing. Adjutant (3) two paces from reverse flank of right centre Company.

"stood on the left of the brigade when in line of contiguous columns, may be
"formed in front of the mass, if each Battalion is right in front the left will be
"the pivot flank of the whole mass.
"When a line of contiguous columns thus forms mass, the Battalions need
"only move perpendicularly, until clear of the columns on the right or left, when
"each Commander will cut off the right angle by the diagonal march."

The leaders of 2, 3, and 4 face about to cover — and front on Brigade Major's word "Steady." Then give word "Dress" to their Companies (2).

(3) pp. 225, 250.   (4) p. 250.   (5) note, p. 63, this book.

No. VII.

Sec. 5, p. 464.

A Brigade in Line of Contiguous, Close, or Quarter Distance Columns, changing Front.

Sec. 5, *p. 464.*   *A Brigade in Line of Contiguous,*

Brigadier.	Commanders of Battalions.	Coverers and Supernumerary Serjeants.
The Brigade will change front to the right flank by echellon on the right Battalion. Bugle or signal. The echellon will wheel to the right, and form line on the right Battalion. Bugle or signal.	All, "*The Brigade will change Front to the Right Flank by Echellon on the Right Battalion.*" All (excepting No. 1), "*By the Right.*" Lieutenants move up (1). "*Quick March.*" Lieutenants leading. All (excepting No. 1) successively, "*Halt*," each on the inner flank, getting in rear of his Supernumerary Serjeant, in a line perpendicular to the new alignment. All, "*The Echellon will wheel to the Right, and form Line on the Right Battalion.*" Commander of No. 1, "*Right wheel.*" Commanders of Nos. 2, 3, 4, "*On the move, Right wheel.*" All, "*Quick March.*" Commander of No. 1, "*Halt,*" when wheeled. Commanders of Nos. 2, 3, 4, "*Forward,*" "*Halt,*" when they have marched up to hands of points. The Battalions will be ordered to dress, if necessary.	Coverers and Supernumerary Serjeants run out and successively mark the ground where the heads of their Battalions are to rest.

REMARKS.——"In these changes of front, the point at which each wheel is
" made must be at the intersection of two straight lines (*d*, *c*, and *e*, *c*), the one
" perpendicular to the old line erected at the inner flank (*d*) of the Battalion, the
" other perpendicular to the new line erected at the point of entry (*e*), where the
" inner flank of the Battalion will rest when the movement is completed. Thus it
" will be found that all the wheeling points, if the columns are correctly halted in
" echellon, will be situated on the same straight line drawn from the point of in-
" tersection of the old and new alignments, and bisecting the angle formed by
" those alignments.
 "In changing front at right angles, it is evident that each Battalion will be
Part of Field Exercise Book authorizing.——(1) p. 461.   (2) p. 250.

Close, or Quarter Distance Columns, changing Front.

Brigade Major.	Post of Mounted Regimental Officers.	
	During Movement.	Movement completed.
Takes much pains to place the Supernumerary Serjeant of front Company of No. 1 (who marks the point of appui) and the Coverer in the correct alignment, as these are the base points on which the other Supernumerary Serjeants marking the inner flank and Coverers form in succession. From the wheeling point he sees to their covering. Should he wish it, he can place a second point (say thirty paces) outside the point of appui as a guide to the distant points (5). Where, however, mounted points are not required, it will be found that this second point is rather an incumbrance than an aid.	Lieutenant - Colonels place themselves, on Brigadier's first caution, close to that flank of their leading Companies which is nearest to wheeling point. When in the new alignment, they shift to the left flank, which becomes the proper pivot of the Battalion the moment the movement is completed. Senior Majors near centre of right flank, in order to avoid shifting (4). Junior Major superintends covering from rear (2). Adjutants near centre of Battalions, on proper reverse flank (the right).	Lieutenant-Colonels (3) on the left (the proper pivot flank) of their several leading Companies, aligning with them. Senior Majors (3) two paces from reverse flank (the right), near the centre of their right wings. Junior Majors (3) two paces from reverse flank, near the centre of their left wings. Adjutants two paces from reverse flank of right centre Company (3).

" formed, when in echellon, at a distance equal to its own breadth and six paces
" from the Battalion next in front of it; and the perpendicular lines from the
" inner flanks of Battalions, and the points of entry, will meet at right angles on
" the wheeling points."

With columns whose depth does not exceed their breadth, it will not be necessary to halt in echellon. Each column will wheel in succession as it arrives perpendicularly in rear of its Supernumerary Serjeant, and when its front is parallel to the new alignment, it will receive the word " Forward," and move up into the new alignment.

(3) pp. 225, 250.   (4) p. 225.   (5) No. 2, p. 220.

No. VIII.

Sec. 5, No. 3, p. 470.

A Brigade in Line of Contiguous, Close, or Quarter Distance Columns changing Front on a Central Battalion (the depth of Columns exceeding their breadth).

Sec. 5, No. 3, p. 470.   A Brigade in Line of Con-
Front on a Central Battalion (the depth

Brigadier.	Commanders of Battalions.	Coverers and Supernumerary Serjeants.
The Brigade will change front to the right by echellon on No. 3 Battalion.	All repeat, "*The Brigade will change Front by echellon on No. 3 Battalion.*" Commander of No. 4, "*No. 4 will advance*," "*By the Right.*" Commander of No. 2, "*No. 2 will retire*," "*Right about face*," "*By the Right.*" Commander of No. 1, the same.	The Supernumerary Serjeant of No. 3 marks the point of appui on right flank of the leading Company of his Battalion. Coverer of No. 3, also Supernumerary Serjeant and Coverer of No. 4, move out and mark the ground where the front of their respective Battalions are to rest, facing the point of appui. Supernumerary Serjeant of front Company of No. 2 will cover, at six paces distance, the base points of No. 3. The Coverer will cover at Company's distance as soon as his column has wheeled clear of the alignment. The Supernumerary Serjeant of front Company of No. 1 will, at six paces distance, cover as soon as he can on base points of No. 2. The Coverer will cover at Company's distance as soon as his column has wheeled clear of the alignment.
Signal or bugle.	No. 4, "*Quick March*," "*Halt,*" on inner flank getting in rear of its Supernumerary Serjeant, in a line perpendicular to the new alignment.	
The echellon will wheel to the right and form line on No. 3 Battalion.	All repeat, "*The echellon will wheel to the right and form line on No. 3 Battalion.*" Commander of No. 3, "*Right wheel.*" Commander of No. 4, "*On the move, right wheel.*"	
Signal or bugle.	All, "*Quick March.*" Commander of No. 3, "*Halt,*" when wheeled into the new alignment. Commander of No. 4, "*Forward,*" "*Halt,*" when up to hands of points. Commander of No. 2, "*Form Fours Right*," when proper front Company is one pace beyond its Supernumerary Serjeant. "*Right wheel,*" as soon as its leading flank has passed its Supernumerary Serjeant. "*Halt,*" "*Front,*" when square with the new alignment. Commander of No. 1, the same.	

Part of Field Exercise Book authorizing.——(1) No. 7, p. 66.   (2) p. 250.

tiguous, Close, or Quarter Distance Columns changing of Columns exceeding their breadth).

Brigade Major.	Post of Mounted Regimental Officers.	
	During Movement.	Movement completed.
Takes pains to place the Supernumerary Serjeant of No. 3 (who marks the point of appui) and the Coverer of No. 3 in the correct alignment; as these constitute the base points on which the other Coverers and Supernumerary Serjeants form in succession.	Each Lieutenant-Colonel close to flank of the leading Company which is nearest to wheeling point. When in the new alignment, he places himself on the left of the front Company, which becomes the proper pivot of the Battalion the moment the movement is completed. Senior Majors of Nos. 3 and 4 near centre of proper right flank to avoid shifting (1). Junior Majors superintend covering from rear (2). Senior Majors of Nos. 1 and 2 from the rear superintend covering of officers (4). Junior Majors near centre of proper right flank, in order to avoid shifting (1).	Lieutenant-Colonels on the left (the proper pivot flank) of their several leading Companies, aligning with them (3). Senior Majors two paces from reverse flank (the right) near the centre of their right wings (3). Junior Majors two paces from reverse flank near the centre of their left wings (3). Adjutant two paces from reverse flank of right centre Company (3).

(3) pp. 225, 250.   (4) Sec. 17, p. 264.   [*For Remarks see over.*]

REMARKS.——" When the depth of the columns exceed their breadth, and the
" Battalions thrown forward are consequently obliged to halt in echellon, those
" which are thrown back must not retire until the rest commence their wheel;
" when the depth of the columns does not exceed their breadth, and the Battalion
" of formation is able to wheel at once, all the Battalions may be put in motion at
" the same time. It may occasionally be necessary to order a Battalion that is
" retiring to mark time until the outer point of the preceding Battalion is
" placed."

Horse Guards, S.W.,
4th April, 1863.

CIRCULAR MEMORANDUM.
General. No. 249.

The two following paragraphs (4 and 5) having been added to Section 5, Part VI., of the "Field Exercise and Evolutions of Infantry," His Royal Highness the Field Marshal Commanding-in-Chief directs that they be inserted in all copies in use in regiments and depôts :—

" 4. *Changing Front on a Central Battalion at Right Angles.*—The Battalion of " Formation, and any Battalion that is thrown forward, will proceed as directed " in No. 3 of this Section. Any Battalion that is thrown back will be retired " till its proper front Company becomes perpendicular to that point in the new " alignment where its outer flank will rest ; the column will then take ground " inwards by fours until it is clear of, and an arm's length beyond, the alignment ; " it will then be ordered to front turn, and wheeled (as described in Part IV., " Section 16,) into position.

" 5. *Changing Front on a Flank Battalion, the remainder thrown back.*—The " Battalion of Formation will proceed as described in Nos. 1—4 of this Section ; " the remainder as directed for the Battalions thrown back in Nos. 3 or 4.

" By command,
" (*Signed*) JAMES YORKE SCARLETT,
" *Adjutant General.*"

Say the change is to the right, the quarter circle on No. 3. The word of command would be—" The Brigade will Change Front to the Right *the Quarter Circle* on No. 3. On its being repeated by Commanders, the Supernumerary Serjeants and Coverers of the leading Company of *all* the Battalions at once move out. Battalions 1 and 2 face about. On signal or bugle, all Battalions, excepting No. 3, move off. Battalions 2 and 1 " Retire" until their proper front Companies are just beyond their not *inner* but *outer* points. " Form Fours Right" and " Halt" on signal or bugle after the command, " The Echellon will Wheel to the Right and Form Line on No. 3 Battalion." Nos. 2 and 1 march on until an arm's length beyond the new alignment, when they will " Front Turn" and " Right Wheel" into position.

It is to be remembered that in oblique changes the Battalions which retire wheel in fours round their *inner* points ; whereas, in changes at right angles, they wheel, front ranks in front, round their *outer* points ; that in oblique changes, only *one* of their points at a time is taken up ; whereas in changes at right angles, *all* the points are taken up at the same time.

No. IX.

Secs. 6 & 7, p. 472.

A Brigade advancing in Line, or retiring in Line.

Brigadier.	Commanders of Battalions.	Coverers and Supernumerary Serjeants.
The Brigade will advance, (say) No. 2 will direct.	All repeat, "*The Brigade will advance, No. 2 will direct.*" All, "*No. — will advance.*" "*By the Centre.*"	Do not move out.
Signal or bugle.	All, "*Quick March.*"	
A Brigade retires on exactly the same principle—but it will not be faced about until everything is ready for its instant march, for it should not stand unnecessarily faced to the rear (3).		

REMARKS.——All conform to the directing Battalion (which is generally a central one), and also conform to it "in subsequent movements, unless another directing Battalion is named. Each Battalion will march by its own centre. The Commander alone will look to the Battalion of direction.

"The centre Serjeant of the Battalion of direction will select points to "march on, under the guidance of the Commanding Officer or Adjutant. These "points should not be too far off, as smoke or dust might conceal them from view. "The direction can be preserved to any distance, by taking fresh points when "necessary in the prolongation of the straight lines passing through the original "points."

Part of Field Exercise Book authorizing.——(1) p. 232.

advancing in Line, or retiring in Line.

Brigade Major.	Post of Mounted Regimental Officers.	
	During Movement.	Movement completed.
May assist Commander and Adjutant of Battalion of direction in selecting points to march on.	Lieutenant-Colonel at first about twenty paces in rear of centre. Unless his be the regulating Battalion, he, or a mounted Officer, remains in rear (2) until the line has advanced twenty or thirty paces, to judge whether the direction of the centre is parallel to that of the regulating Battalion. " Any deviation from the " proper direction will be " made apparent by the " increase or decrease of " the intervals between " Battalions," which the Majors on the wings should instantly by signs make known to Commanding Officer. Senior Major six paces in rear of centre of right wing. Junior Major six paces in rear of centre of left wing. Adjutant six paces in rear of colours (1).	Lieutenant-Colonel (1) about twenty paces in rear of centre. Senior Major (1) six paces in rear of centre of right wing. Junior Major (1) six paces in rear of centre of left wing. Adjutant (1) six paces in rear of colours.

The direction of the regulating Battalion should not be altered. The centre Serjeants of the other Battalions will also select points to move on, but their direction will be altered when any deviation from the proper direction is made apparent by the increase or decrease of the intervals between Battalions.

If any part of the Brigade falls in rear of the directing Battalion, the latter must be ordered to " *step short,*" until the rest come up.

Battalions marching over heights or across valleys, require more time than those moving on a level; the latter should therefore be ordered to " *step short.*"

(2) p. 236.   (3) IV. p. 229.

No. X.

Sec. 8, p. 473.

A Brigade advancing or retiring in Line of Contiguous Columns.

Sec. 8, p. 473. A Brigade advancing or

Brigadier.	Commanders of Battalions.	Coverers and Supernumerary Serjeants.
The Brigade will advance, (say) No. 2 will direct.	All, "*The Brigade will advance, No. 2 will direct.*" Commanders of No. 2 and of No. 1, "*By the Left.*" Commanders of Nos. 3 and 4, "*By the Right.*" Lieutenants lead (1).	Do not move out.
Bugle or signal.	All, "*Quick March.*"	
The Brigade will be halted.	All, "*The Brigade will be halted.*"	
Bugle or signal.	All, "*Halt,*" "*Dress,*" if necessary.	

REMARKS.——The Lieutenants of 3 and 4 move up and lead (1) and cover *in their relative positions.*

The directing Battalion marches by its proper pivot flank (the left); the remaining Battalion by the flank nearest to the directing Battalion, preserving six paces and dressing from it.

A retirement is conducted on exactly the same principles as in an advance. The Senior Majors (not the Juniors) would see from the rear (the proper front) that their Officers covered. The order would be, "*The Brigade will retire,*"—or,

| The Brigade will be halted and fronted. | All, "*The Brigade will be halted and fronted.*" Commander of No. 2, "*Halt—front.*" Commanders of other Battalions, "*Halt—front,*" at such time as may be necessary to bring their proper front Companies in line with the front of the Battalion of direction. Some may have to give the order, "*Front turn,*" "*Halt.*" | Supernumerary Serjeant of proper front Company of No. 2, and Coverer, give base points at arm's length from front Company. The Supernumerary Serjeant and Coverer of leading Companies of other Battalions cover in succession. |

REMARKS.——No signal or bugle (after the caution) for a simultaneous halt and front.

If in retiring, the Battalions have retained their relative positions, they will

Part of Field Exercise Book authorizing.——(1) 8, p. 66.

retiring in Line of Contiguous Columns.

Brigade Major.	Post of Mounted Regimental Officers.	
	During Movement.	Movement completed.
From the rear of No. 2, names a point on which the Captain of the leading Company is to march, and watches the movement. By the crowding in or opening from adjoining Brigade, judges whether the line of direction ought to be altered. All depends upon which is the directing Brigade of the Division.	Lieutenant-Colonels on the left (2) of their respective Battalions (the proper pivot). Senior Majors near centre of right wings on reverse flank (2), seeing (should that flank be next to the directing Battalion) that the leader of the leading Company keeps the six paces. If it be the Lieutenant-Colonel who is next to the directing Battalion, he will watch that the leader preserves the six paces to avoid unnecessary shifting (1). The Junior Majors in rear (2) of Officers leading Companies, looking to the covering. Adjutants near centre of proper reverse flank (2).	Each Lieutenant-Colonel (2) on pivot flank of and aligning with leading Company. Each Senior Major (2) two paces from reverse flank of centre of right wing. Each Junior Major (2) two paces from reverse flank of centre of left wing. Adjutants (2) two paces from reverse flank of right centre Company.

Dressing after the halt ought not to be necessary. If it be necessary, No. 2 will give base foot points, on which the Supernumerary Serjeants and Coverers of leading Companies of other Battalions will form.

if for a short distance, "*The Brigade will retire, Battalions retaining their relative positions.*" (Say) "*No. 2 direct.*" In the latter case, the leading Company of each Battalion will not be ordered to move in line with that of the regulating Battalion.

From point of appui (the left of front Company of No. 2) dresses points.		

halt and front together, in which case the bugle would be sounded for this movement to be performed simultaneously.

(2) pp. 225, 250.

No. XI.

Sec. 9, p. 474.

Brigade advancing or retiring in Line of Quarter Distance Columns, at Deploying Distance.

Sec. 9, p. 474.   *A Brigade advancing or retiring in*

Brigadier.	Commanders of Battalions.	Coverers and Supernumerary Serjeants.
The Brigade will advance, (say) No. 2 will direct. Signal or bugle.	All, "*The Brigade will advance, No. 2 will direct.*" Commander of No. 2 and of No. 1, "*By the Left.*" Commanders of Nos. 3 and 4, "*By the Right.*" Lieutenants lead (2). All, "*Quick March.*"	Do not move out.
The Brigade will retire, (say) No. 2 direct.	"When a Brigade is ordered to retire, similar arrangements will be made facing to the rear, the Majors of the proper rear wings of Battalions or the Adjutants, as may be required, moving in line with the proper rear Companies, and keeping their dressing on the proper rear rank of the proper rear Company of the Battalion of direction. On the words *Halt—Front,* or *Front—Turn,* the Majors of the front wings, or the Adjutants, as may be required, will move up to preserve the distances in the front alignment, all dressing on the proper front Company of the Battalion of direction. It will usually be found convenient to name the deepest column in the Brigade to direct when retreating."	

REMARKS.——The Lieutenants of Nos. 3 and 4 (2) lead the Companies. All conform to directing Battalion, and conform to it during subsequent movements, until another directing Battalion is named (3). All distances are taken and preserved from it.

" When the columns are left in front, the same rules apply, the flanks being " reversed, and the Junior Major leading when required."

Part of Field Exercise Book authorizing.——(1) pp. 250, 225.

Line of Quarter Distance Columns, at Deploying Distance.

Brigade Major.	Post of Mounted Regimental Officers.	
	During Movement.	Movement completed.
From rear and left of No. 2, names a point on which the Captains of No. 2 are to march.	Lieutenant-Colonels on the left, the proper pivot flank (1). Senior Majors of No. 2 on reverse flank (the right), near centre of right wing (1). Senior Major of No. 1 on the inner flank, next to the Captain of the leading Company, regulating the advance so as to preserve deploying distance and six paces from No. 2. Senior Majors* of Nos. 3 and 4 on the inner flank, each near to the Lieutenant of his leading Company, seeing that six paces are preserved from the Adjutant on his right. Junior Majors of Nos. 1 and 2 (1) from rear, attending to covering of Captains. Junior Majors of Nos. 3 and 4 from rear, attending to covering of Lieutenants (in their relative positions if the advance is short) (4). Adjutants of Nos. 2, 3, and 4 marking the deploying distance of their respective Battalions. Adjutant of No. 1 near centre of proper reverse flanks (1).	Lieutenant-Colonel on (1) pivot flank of leading Company. Senior Major (1) two paces from reverse flank of centre of right wing. Junior Major (1) two paces from reverse flank of centre of left wing. Adjutant (1) two paces from reverse flank of right centre Company.

* As Senior Majors "regulate the march of their columns," it is clear that the Juniors from the rear should attend to the covering of the Officers rather than "superintend the direction of the columns," p. 250. The Junior Major, however, superintends the direction of his column when it regulates and marches on a fixed point.

If we suppose the point of entry (the point of appui) for the Brigade to be on the left, it is clear that distances would be taken from the left, and that when ordered to deploy, the Battalions (as they are supposed to be right in front) would deploy on their rear Companies (see also remarks, p. 132).

"Mounted Officers giving points must not fall back to their posts until dismissed by signal from the Brigade Major" (p. 451).

(2) 8, p. 66.   (3) p. 275.   (4) 2, p. 473.

No. XII.

Sec. 10, p. 475.

A Brigade formed in Line of Double Columns, at Deploying Distance, advancing or retiring.

Sec. 10, p. 475. *A Brigade formed in Line of Double*

Brigadier.	Commanders of Battalions.	Coverers and Supernumerary Serjeants.
The Brigade will advance, (say) No. 2 direct, (suppose double column of subdivisions). Signal or bugle.	All, "*The Brigade will advance, No. 2 direct.*" Commanders of No. 2 and No. 1, "*By the Left.*" Commanders of Nos. 3 and 4, "*By the Right.*" All, "*Quick March.*"	Do not move out.
The Brigade will retire, (say) No. 2 direct.*		

* Precisely the same arrangement will be made as for the advance. All will be faced about; alignment will be preserved from the proper rear rank of the rear subdivision of the directing Battalion.

REMARKS.——Should the Line be ordered to dress on the directing Battalion, its centre Serjeant and the Coverers of the two leading Companies (VI., p. 230) will give points at arm's length in front of the line on which the columns are to dress. The other centre Serjeants and Coverers of leading Companies facing inwards towards the point of appui, cover on them.

Part of Field Exercise Book authorizing.——(1) p. 225.   (2) p. 288.

Columns, at Deploying Distance, advancing or retiring. 67

Brigade Major.	Post of Mounted Regimental Officers.	
	During Movement.	Movement completed.
From the rear of the left (the proper pivot flank) of No. 2 gives a point for Captain of leading subdivision of its left wing to march on, and watches that the other Battalions do not get out of the alignment.	Lieutenant-Colonels (1) near the left (the proper pivot) flank, aligning with front subdivisions. Senior Major (1) of No. 2 in rear of the second Company from the front of the left wing of No. 2 Battalion, seeing that Captains march correctly on the given points. Junior Major (2) of No. 2 accompanies the movement at deploying distance of left wing. Junior Major of No. 1 on left of his columns, preserving wing distance and six paces from Adjutant of No. 2. Senior Major of No. 3 on right of leading subdivision of the right wing, preserving deploying distance of right wing, and six paces from Junior Major of No. 2. Senior Major of No. 4 on right of leading subdivision of right wing, preserving deploying distance of right wing, and six paces from Adjutant of No. 3. Senior Major of No 1, and Junior Majors of Nos. 3 and 4, from the rear look to covering of Officers (4).	Lieutenant-Colonels (1) on the left (the proper pivot) flank, aligning with front subdivisions. Senior Majors near centre of right wings. Junior Majors (1) near centre of left wings. Adjutants (1) near rear of outer flanks.
	The Adjutant of No. 1 follows in rear of column (2). The Adjutant of No. 2 accompanies the movement at deploying distance of right wing (5). The Adjutants of Nos. 3 and 4 accompany the movement at deploying distance of left wing (5). N.B.—This is on supposition that column is at half distance—but double column at quarter distance would generally be formed as represented in Plates LIX. and LX.	

The points being dressed, the Battalions are moved up to them.
On the Brigade Major giving the word " *Steady*," the points resume their positions in Battalion.
Mounted Officers giving points must not fall back to their posts until dismissed by signal from the Brigade Major (3).

(3) p. 451.   (4) note, p. 63, this book.   (5) p. 475.

No. XIII.

Sec. 11, p. 476.

A Brigade in Line advancing in Open Columns from the Flanks of Battalions, or in Double Column from the Centre of Battalions.

Sec. 11, p. 476.   *A Brigade in Line advancing in Open Column from the*

Brigadier.	Commanders of Battalions.	Coverers and Supernumerary Serjeants.
The Brigade will advance in open column of Companies from the (say) right of Battalions. (Say) No. 1 will direct. Signal or bugle.	All, "*The Brigade will advance in Open Column of Companies from the Right of Battalions.*" "*No. 1 will direct.*" "*Right Company to the Front, Remaining Companies on the move, Right Wheel*" (1). All, "*Quick March,*" "*Forward,*" when square in column (1). No. 1 advances by left (2). Nos. 2, 3, and 4 by right (2). Their Lieutenants lead Companies (8).	The Coverers of leading Companies shift on caution (4).

REMARKS.——No. 1 will march by the left (the proper pivot) flank—the remaining Battalions by the right, the flank nearest to No. 1 (the regulating Battalion), on the same principle as when in contiguous columns (2). The point

| The Brigade will advance in double column of subdivisions (or Companies) from the centre of Battalions, (say) No. 4 Battalion will direct. Signal or bugle. | All, "*The Brigade will advance in Double Column of Subdivisions from the Centre of Battalions. No. 4 Battalion will direct.*" "*Two Centre Subdivisions to the Front, Remaining Subdivisions on the move, Inwards wheel.*" All, "*Quick March,*" "*Forward,*" when square in column (6), "*By the Left.*" | Coverers of the flank Companies mark where subdivisions wheel (12). |

Columns from the Flanks of Battalions, or in Double Centre of Battalions.

Brigade Major.	Post of Mounted Regimental Officers.	
	During Movement.	Movement completed.
Names a point on which No. 1 Battalion is to march. From the right of line looks to the dressing of the leading Companies of Battalions.	Lieutenant-Colonel near pivot flank of leading Company (3). Senior Major of No. 1 in rear of the pivot flank of second Company from front (3). Other Senior Majors on the right (the inner) flank of their Battalions, to preserve six paces from the Adjutants on their right (2). Junior Majors superintend the second wheel, and then follow in rear of their respective columns, looking to covering of Officers (9). Adjutants on left of their respective Battalions, preserving deploying distance.	Lieutenant-Colonels on proper pivot flank of their leading Companies (3). Senior Major of No. 1 Battalion in rear of pivot flank of second Company from the front (3). Senior Majors of Nos. 2, 3, and 4, on the right of their respective Battalions, to see that six paces are preserved from Adjutant on the right (4). Junior Majors (3) two paces from reverse flank centre of left wing. Adjutant (3) two paces from centre of reverse flank of right centre Company.

of appui would be on the right of No. 1, should the columns be ordered to deploy on the front Company of No. 1 (10).

| Names a point on which No. 4 Battalion is to march.

From the left of line looks to dressing of leading Companies of Battalions. | Lieutenant - Colonels near left (proper pivot) flank of their leading subdivision (7).
Junior Major of No. 4 in rear of the left (the pivot) flank of the second subdivision from the front (3).
All other Junior Majors on the left flank of leading subdivision, to preserve wing distance, and six paces from Adjutants on the left.
Senior Majors superintend second wheel, and then follow in rear of their several columns, looking to covering of Officers (9).
Adjutants on the right, preserving wing distance for their right wings (5). | Lieutenant-Colonels on pivot flank of their leading Companies (3).
All Majors in rear of their respective wings (9).
Adjutants in rear, between them (11). |

For Remarks and Part of Field Exercise Book authorizing see p. **72.**

REMARKS.——All Battalions advance by their proper left. Should they be ordered to deploy, the centre of No. 4 would become the point of appui, which would be marked by its centre Serjeant (12).

Part of Field Exercise Book authorizing.——(1) p. 281.   (2) No. 1, p. 475.
(3) p. 225.   (4) p. 282.   (5) p. 475.   (6) Sec. 10, p. 285.   (7) Plate XXX.
(8) 8, p. 66.   (9) p. 286.   (10) p. 315, Plate XXXIV.   (11) Old usage.
(12) p. 324.

No. XIV.

Sec. 12, p. 476.

A Brigade retiring in Open Column of Companies, from the one Flank of Battalions in rear of the other, or from both Flanks of Battalions in rear of their Centres.

74   Sec. 12, p. 476.   *A Brigade retiring in Open Column of the other, or from both Flanks*

Brigadier.	Commanders of Battalions.	Coverers and Supernumerary Serjeants.
The Brigade will retire in open column of Companies from the (say) left in rear of the right of Battalions, (say) No. 1 will direct. Signal or bugle.	All, "*The Brigade will retire in Open Column of Companies from the Left in Rear of the Right of Battalions,*" "*No. 1 will direct.*" All, "*No. — retire by Companies from the Left in Rear of the Right.*" All, "*Quick March.*" No. 1 retires by proper left (3). Nos. 2, 3, and 4, by proper right (3). Lieutenants lead Companies (7).	Coverer of No. 1 Company falls back and gives point in rear of Coverer of No. 2, for Companies to wheel on (1).

REMARKS.——During the retirement, No. 1 will march by its present right, its proper pivot flank (3).

The other Battalions by the present left (the proper right) (3).

It would be well to bear in mind that this retirement is, in its details, the advance of the Brigade in open columns from the right flank of Battalions, No. 1 directing (p. 70, this book), all *faced about*—the mounted points aligning with the leading Companies, and the Junior Majors taking the duties the Seniors had performed during its advance.

Part of Field Exercise Book authorizing.—(1) p. 287.   (2) p. 479.

Companies, from the one Flank of Battalions in rear of of Battalions in rear of their Centres.

Brigade Major.	Post of Mounted Regimental Officers.	
	During Movement.	Movement completed.
The Brigade Major, having given the direction in which No. 1 Battalion is to retire, moves to the flank of its leading Company, to superintend the alignment of the leading Companies of all the Battalions.	Lieutenant-Colonels, at first, near centre and wheeling point. Junior Major of No. 1 on present right (proper left) in rear of pivot flank of the second leading Company, to superintend the direction (4). Other Junior Majors (5) on proper right (present left) of leading Companies, preserving six paces from the Adjutants on their right (present left). Senior Majors superintend the second wheels, and then follow in rear of their respective columns, looking to covering of Officers (6). All Adjutants on their present right mark deploying distance of their Battalions.	Lieutenant-Colonels (4) on proper pivot flank of leading Companies. The Junior Major of directing Battalion on proper left (present right) in rear of pivot flank of the second leading Company, to superintend the direction (4). Other Junior Majors on proper right flank, (inner, present left,) preserving six paces. All Senior Majors in rear of their respective columns, looking to covering of Officers (6). Adjutants on their present right mark deploying distance of their Battalions.

Had the Battalion on the proper left directed, the Junior Majors of 1, 2, and 3 (as their left wings led) would have preserved deploying distance and six paces.

Had a central Battalion directed, the Junior Majors on its proper right would have preserved the deploying distance and six paces. The Junior Majors on the proper left of the directing Battalion would have preserved the six paces from the Adjutants (2).

(3) No. 1, sec. 8, p. 471.   (4) p. 225.   (5) No. 5, p. 472.   (6) p. 286.   (7) 8, p. 66.

No. XV.

Sec. 13, p. 477.

A Brigade advancing in Double Column of Companies from the Centre, or retiring by Companies from both Flanks in rear of the Centre.

Sec. 13, p. 477. A Brigade advancing in Double Companies from both Flanks

Brigadier.	Commanders of Battalions.	Coverers and Supernumerary Serjeants.
The Brigade will advance* in double column of Companies from its centre.	All, "*The Brigade will advance in Double Column of Companies from its Centre.*" Commander of No. 2, "*Left Company to the Front,*" (1) "*remaining Companies on the move, Left wheel.*" Commander of No. 3, "*Right Company to the Front, remaining Companies on the move, Right wheel.*" Commander of No. 1, "*Companies on the move, Left wheel.*" Commander of No. 4, "*Companies on the move, Right wheel.*"	Coverer of right Company of 3 and 4 change flank. Coverer of No. 2 Company falls to rear (4).
Signal or bugle.	All, "*Quick March.*" All, "*Forward,*" when square in column. Nos. 1 and 2 march "*By the Left,*" (the inner flank,)	
* For the retirement, see p. 82.	3 and 4 "*By the Right.*"	

REMARKS.——The proper left centre Battalion (No. 3) directs, unless the contrary is ordered.

All march in column by inner flank; six paces between the columns.

"The Lieutenants lead and keep the distance of their own Companies, with-
" out regard to the position of the corresponding Companies in the double column,
" of which the two leading Companies only are required to keep in line."

"When the number of Battalions in a Brigade is even, the inner Companies
" of the two centre Battalions will be considered as the centre; when the number
" of Battalions is uneven, the two centre Companies of the centre Battalion will
" be considered the centre of the Brigade, without reference to the strength of
" Battalions, or number of Companies in them."

Part of Field Exercise Book authorizing.——(1) p. 281.

Column of Companies from the Centre, or retiring by in rear of the Centre.

Brigade Major.	Post of Mounted Regimental Officers.	
	During Movement.	Movement completed.
Places himself in rear of the right flank of left centre Battalion, (No. 3,) names distant point for marching on, and may move in rear of the Lieutenant who leads the double column.	Lieutenant-Colonels (3) near proper pivot flank of their respective leading Companies. Senior Major of No. 3 from rear of Lieutenant who leads, superintends direction of march, unless the Brigade Major does so. Senior Major of 4, and Junior Majors of 1 and 2, from rear of second Lieutenant from the front, superintend covering (3). Senior Majors of 1 and 2, and Junior Majors of 3 and 4, after superintending the second wheels, follow in rear, superintending the covering of Lieutenants (2). Adjutants in rear, or where most useful (2).	Lieutenant-Colonels on proper pivot flank (3) of their leading Companies. Senior Major of No. 3, to superintend direction, will move in rear of the Lieutenant who leads, unless Brigade Major does so. Senior Major of No. 4, and Junior Majors of Nos. 1 and 2, in rear of the inner flank of the second Company from the front (3). Senior Majors of Nos. 1 and 2, and Junior Majors of Nos. 3 and 4, superintend covering of Lieutenants from the rear of their respective battalions (2). Adjutants in rear, or on reverse flank,—where most useful (2).

Had the advance been from the two centre Companies of a Battalion, only room would have been left between the columns for the Lieutenants to have moved up and led on the inner flanks. The colours would have dropped to the rear.

When the Brigade in double column advances with other Brigades, Staff Officers, or the Adjutants of the outer Battalions, preserve distance for the whole Brigade " in precisely the same manner as the deploying distances of Battalions " in double column are preserved in a Brigade."

" The Major or Brigade Major superintending the direction of the column, " will be responsible for the distance of the inner half of the Brigade, when it is " not the regulating Brigade."

(2) On principle p. 286.   (3) p. 225.   (4) p. 282.

No. XVI.

Sec. 13, No. 2, p. 478.

ade retiring in Double Column of Companies from both Flanks in rear of Centre.

Sec. 13, No. 2, p. 478.   The Brigade retiring in rear of

Brigadier.	Commanders of Battalions.	Coverers and Supernumerary Serjeants.
The Brigade will retire by Companies from both flanks in rear of its centre. Signal or bugle.	All, "*The Brigade will retire by Companies from both flanks in rear of its Centre.*" Commander of No. 1, "*Retire by Companies from Right, in Rear of the Centre of Brigade.*" Commander of No. 4, "*Retire by Companies from Left, in Rear of the Centre of Brigade.*" The Captains of right flank Company of No. 1 and left flank Company of No. 4, "*Right about Face.*" "*Quick March.*" Commander of No. 2, (on left Company of No. 1, approaching right Company of No. 2,) "*Retire by Companies from Right, in Rear of Centre of Brigade.*" Commander of No. 3, (on right Company of No. 4, nearing left Company of No. 3,) "*Retire by Companies from the Left, in Rear of Centre of Brigade.*"	The Coverer of left Company of No. 2 Battalion gives a point in rear of his Captain (1), at a distance which ought to be equal to the breadth of the strongest Company of the right wing of the Brigade, and three paces. The Coverer of the right Company of No. 3 Battalion falls back and gives a point in rear of the Covering Serjeant (1) of the next Company (facing towards him), at a distance which ought to be equal to the breadth of the strongest Company, and three paces of the left wing of the Brigade.

REMARKS.——This is almost exactly the advancing double column described in page 78 of this book, *faced about*.

The proper left wing of the Brigade will direct, unless the proper right wing is strongest.

The columns march by inner flanks, six paces between columns; the Lieutenants lead, and keep the distance of the Companies respectively preceding them, without regard to the position of the corresponding Companies in the double column.

As the weakest wing will sooner than the other have completed its formation in column, it will mark time or halt (by order of Commanders), until the stronger wing is in column, and the two centre Companies of the Brigade align, when the Lieutenant of the leading Company of the weakest wing, will preserve "his *relative* position with the stronger wing" (the directing wing). Thus "the proper

Part of Field Exercise Book authorizing.——(1) p. 287

Double Column of Companies from both Flanks in 83
its Centre.

Brigade Major.	Post of Mounted Regimental Officers.	
	During Movement.	Movement completed.
Places himself in front of the right flank of right Company of No. 3; names distant point, and may move in rear of the Lieutenant who leads the double column.	Lieut.-Colonels may be near wheeling point, subsequently, on proper pivot flank of leading Company (2). Junior Major of No. 4, from rear of Lieutenant who leads, superintends direction of march (3), unless the Brigade Major superintends. Junior Major (2) of No. 3, and Senior Majors of Nos. 1 and 2, from rear of their second leading Lieutenants, see that Lieutenants cover. Senior Majors of Nos. 4 and 3, and Junior Majors of Nos. 1 and 2, superintend the wheel (3). Adjutants in rear, or where most useful (3).	Lieut.-Colonels may be on proper pivot flank of their leading Companies (2). Senior Majors of Nos. 1 and 2, and Junior of No. 3 in present rear of inner flank of second leading Company (2). Junior Major of No. 4, from rear of Lieutenant who leads, superintends direction of march (3). Junior Majors of Nos. 1 and 2, and Seniors of Nos. 4 and 3, and Adjutants, follow in rear of their respective Battalions; the Major looking to covering of Lieutenants (3).

" wheeling distance of the Companies will be kept," the two centre Companies of
" the Brigade will always be in a line ready to form a base when the column is
" halted and fronted."

When the Brigade in double columns retires with other Brigades, Staff Officers or the Adjutants of the outer Battalions preserve distance for the whole Brigade, aligning with the leading Companies in precisely the same manner as the deploying distances of Battalions retiring in double columns are preserved in a Brigade.

" The Major or Brigade Major superintending the direction of the column,
" will be responsible for the distance of the inner half of the Brigade, when it is
" not the regulating Battalion."

The Lieutenants who lead the Battalions which follow, preserve a distance between Battalions equal to the breadth of the retiring Company which precedes them, plus six paces (4).

(2) p. 225.   (3) p. 292, IV. p. 219.   (4) V. p. 447.

No. XVII.

Sec. 14, p. 479.

Brigade standing in Double Column of Companies forming Line to the Front (the whole Brigade in one Double Column).

Sec. 14, p. 479. *A Brigade in Double Column of Com-
one Double*

Brigadier.	Commanders of Battalions.	Coverers and Supernumerary Serjeants.
The Brigade will form line on the leading Companies by echellon. [When echellon is formed,] Signal or bugle. Or, the Brigade will form line on the leading Companies; the centre Battalions by echellon, the other Battalions by quarter distance.* Or, the Brigade will close at the double to quarter distance on the two leading Companies, and then deploy. * The general run of ground makes this the more usual movement.	All, "*The Brigade will form Line on the Leading Companies by Echellon.*" Commander of No. 3, "*No. 3, Front Company stand fast, remaining Companies Four Paces on the Right backwards wheel,*" "*Quick March.*" Commander of No. 2, the same, excepting that the Companies wheel back on the left, "*Quick March.*" Commander of No. 4, "*No. 4, on the Right, Four Paces backwards wheel.*" "*Quick March.*" Commander of No. 1, "*No. 1, on the Left, Four Paces backwards wheel,*" "*Quick March.*" (2). All, "*Quick March.*" Nos. 1 and 4 move to where their respective left and right flanks are to rest in the alignment, and then their Companies successively wheel into line (3).	Supernumerary Serjeant of leading Company of No. 3 marks point of appui on the right flank. Its Coverer is dressed in the required alignment by the Brigade Major. These two constitute the base points of the Brigade. Supernumerary and Coverer of leading Companies of No. 2 cover on base points. Other Coverers in succession.

REMARKS.——The right of No. 3 is the point of appui, and for this reason :—Were the Brigade ordered to advance in column, and were no instructions given to the contrary, No. 3 would direct.

Part of Field Exercise Book authorizing.——(1) 1st, p. 350. (2) p. 299.

panies forming Line to the Front (the whole Brigade in Column).

Brigade Major.	Post of Mounted Regimental Officers.	
	During Movement.	Movement completed.
The right flank of No. 3 being the point of appui (see remarks), the Brigade Major places a Supernumerary Serjeant of No. 1 Company of that Battalion, to mark it, and then places the Coverer of the same Company in a line with the distant point previously determined on by the General. The Brigade Major then shifts to beyond the Coverer to determine upon a distant point in the opposite direction, unless there be a second Staff Officer to take that duty.	Lieutenant-Colonels of Nos. 3 and 2 near the centre of their respective Battalions watching movements (5). Lieutenant-Colonels of Nos. 4 and 1 near the inner flanks of their respective echellons (6). Senior Major of No. 3, and Junior of No. 2, on their respective inner flanks dressing Coverers (5). Junior Major of No. 3, and Senior of No. 2, about six paces in rear of their respective outer wings (5). Senior Major of No. 4, and Junior of No. 1, in rear of Officer leading the inner Company of their respective Battalions (6). Subsequently dress Coverers from inner flank. Junior Major of No. 4, and Senior of No. 1, about six paces in rear of centre of outer wings (5). Adjutants of Nos. 3 and 2 on outer flank, marking the deploying distances of their Battalions (2). Adjutants of Nos. 4 and 1 in rear of centre; (6) subsequently on outer flank, marking deploying distance (1).	Lieutenant-Colonels (4) about 20 paces in rear of centre. Senior Majors (4) six paces in rear of centre of right wings. Junior Majors (4) six paces in rear of centre of left wings. Adjutants (4) six paces in rear of colours (4).

If done in quarter distance, Nos. 1 and 4 close on their leading Companies—move across the alignment in fours (generally diagonally), and then deploy.

(3) No. V., p. 343.   (4) p. 232.   (5) Plate XL.   (6) Plate XXXIX.

No. XVIII.

Sec. 14, p. 480.

Brigade in Double Column of Companies forming Line to a Flank.

Sec. 14, p. 480. A Brigade in Double Column

Brigadier.	Commanders of Battalions.	Coverers and Supernumerary Serjeants.
The Brigade will be halted. Signal or bugle.	All, "*The Brigade will be halted.*" All, "*Halt.*"	Coverers of leading Companies of 1 and 2 run out (1) on their Battalions being ordered to wheel into line.
The Brigade will form line to the right.	All, "*The Brigade will form Line to the Right.*"	Coverers of all Companies of 3 and 4 take the places of their Captains when these change their flanks (2).
Companies of right wing of Brigade will close upon Captains.	All, "*Companies of Right Wing of Brigade will close upon Captains.*" Commanders of Nos. 1 and 2, "*Battalions close upon Captains,*" "*Quick March.*"	Supernumerary Serjeants and Coverers of leading Companies of 3 and 4 give base points, covering at arm's length from the general alignment.
The right wing of Brigade will wheel into line. The left wing will form line to the reverse flank.	All, "*The Right Wing of Brigade will wheel into Line. The Left Wing will form Line to the Right Flank.*" Commanders of Nos. 1 and 2, "*Right wheel into Line.*" Commander of No. 3, "*No. 3, By the Right;*" (subsequently, calculating for six paces beyond No. 2,) "*Form Line to Reverse Flank.*" Commander of No. 4, "*No. 4, By the Right;*" (subsequently, calculating for six paces beyond No. 3,) "*Form Line to Reverse Flank.*"	Line formed obliquely to a flank. See remarks.
Signal or bugle.	All, "*Quick March.*"	

Part of Field Exercise Book authorizing.——(1) p. 227.   (2) p. 303.   (3) No. 8, p. 450.

of Companies forming Line to a Flank. 91

Brigade Major.	Post of Mounted Regimental Officers.	
	During Movement.	Movement completed.
From the front and right of the leading Company of No. 2 sees to the covering of the Captains of the right wing of the Brigade. He may make the Supernumerary Serjeant and Coverer of the leading Company of No. 3 give the base points on which the other Coverers of left wing are to cover. Should the wheel into line of the right wing be previously completed, he can use the two outer Coverers of No. 2 (3).	Lieut.-Colonels edging near to centre of their Battalions, watching movement. Senior Majors of Nos. 1 and 2 dress pivots from right (1). Senior Majors of Nos. 3 and 4 dress Coverers from right (4). Junior Majors of 1 and 2 in rear of their respective wings. Junior Majors of 3 and 4 on flank of their left wings. Adjutants of 3 and 4 move out to mark the distant flank of their respective Battalions (2).	Lieutenant-Colonel (6) about twenty paces in rear of centre. Senior Major (6) six paces in rear of centre of right wing. Junior Major (6) six paces in rear of centre of left wing. Adjutants (6) six paces in rear of colours.

(4) p. 304.   (5) 3, p. 261.   (6) p. 232.   (7) 2, VI., p. 220.   (8) p. 307.
[*For Remarks see p.* 92.

REMARKS.——If to a flank, in an oblique direction, the Coverers of the inner wing (we suppose the right Battalions, 2 and 1,) will run out in succession, and take up distance and covering for the pivot flank of their respective Companies, the Junior Majors covering them from the front. The Coverer of the leading Company of No. 2 sometimes takes distance from the point on which the column originally marched (5). Frequently the Brigade Major places this point, also a second point outside the other, as a guide to the distant point and the Coverers (7). The Companies of the right wing will then receive the word from their Commanders, " Form Fours Right," "March on your Coverers,"(5) and be wheeled by Battalions into line, on the same signal by which the left wing of the Brigade moves off.

The Battalions of the left wing will advance, receiving the order from their Commanders. " Form Oblique Line to Reverse Flank." The leading Company will at once change direction so as to move on a line parallel to the new alignment. Its Captain shifts his flank during the wheel, and when six paces beyond left flank of No. 2, gives words, " Right wheel—Double—Forward—Halt " (4). The remaining Companies of 3 and 4 form to the reverse flank in like manner; the Captains change direction when they arrive at the same spot, and shift their flanks during the wheel (8).

When the Brigade forms part of a Division, only under very peculiar circumstances could it happen that this movement would be required.

No. XIX.

Sec. 15, p. 483.

A Brigade (from Line) advancing in Open Column of Companies from either Flank, or retiring by Companies from one Flank in rear of the other.

Sec. 15, p. 483. *A Brigade (from Line) advancing in by Companies from one*

Brigadier.	Commanders of Battalions.	Coverers and Supernumerary Serjeants.
The Brigade will advance in open column of Companies from (say) its right. Signal or bugle.	All, "*The Brigade will advance in Open Column of Companies from its Right.*" Commander of No. 1, "*Right Company to the Front* (1), *Remaining Companies on the Move, Right wheel.*" Commanders of Nos. 2, 3, and 4, "*Companies on the Move, Right wheel.*" All, "*Quick March.*" All Battalions advance by the left.	Do not move out.

REMARKS.——" The Captain of the leading Company of each Battalion " (except the first) will be responsible for his Company's wheeling distance, and " six paces from the Battalion in front of him."

| The Brigade will retire in open column of Companies from (say) the left, in rear of its right. As there is no simultaneous movement, there is no signal. | All, "*The Brigade will retire in Open Column of Companies from the Left, in Rear of its Right.*" Commander of No. 4, "*Retire by Companies from the Left, in Rear of the Right of the Brigade.*" Commanders of Nos. 3, 2, and 1, in succession, "*Retire by Companies from Left, in Rear of Right of the Brigade.*" All Captains commanding Companies, in succession from the left, "*Right about Face.*" All Battalions retire by the proper left. | Coverer of right flank Company of No. 1 (2) gives a point in rear of the Captain of No. 2 Company, facing towards him, for all the Companies of the Brigade to wheel on, calculating for the strongest Company in the Brigade. |

REMARKS.——" The Captain of the leading Company of each Battalion " will be responsible for the wheeling distance of the Company which precedes " him and six paces."

Open Column of Companies from either Flank, or retiring Flank in rear of the other.

Brigade Major.	Post of Mounted Regimental Officers.	
	During Movement.	Movement completed.
From the rear of the left flank of No. 1 Company of No. 1 Battalion, names distant point for its Captain to march upon.	Each Lieutenant-Colonel (5) near pivot of his leading Company. Each Senior Major in rear of pivot flank of his second Company from the front, to superintend direction (5). Each Junior Major superintends the second wheel of his Companies (3). Each Adjutant near wheeling point, or where most wanted (6).	Each Lieutenant-Colonel (5) aligning with his leading Company on its pivot flank. Each Senior Major (5) in rear of pivot flank of second Company from the front, to superintend direction. Each Junior Major two paces on reverse flank of centre of left wing (5). Each Adjutant on reverse flank, two paces from right centre Company (5).
From the front and left of the proper right Company of No. 1 Battalion, names distant point for Captain of left flank Company to march on.	Each Lieutenant-Colonel (5) near proper pivot flank of his leading Company. Each Junior Major (5) following pivot flank of the Company next to the leading Company, to superintend direction. The Senior Major superintends the wheel (4). Adjutant near wheeling point, or where most required (6).	Each Lieutenant-Colonel (5) aligning with leading Company on its proper pivot flank. Each Senior Major (5) two paces from centre on proper reverse flank of right wing. Each Junior Major (5) following proper pivot flank of the Company next to the leading Company, to superintend direction. Each Adjutant on proper reverse flank, two paces from right centre Company.

Part of Field Exercise Book authorizing.——(1) p. 281.   (2) p. 287.   (3) On principle, Plate XXX.   (4) On principle, Plate XXXI.   (5) p. 225.   (6) IV., p. 219.

No. XX.

Sec. 16, p. 483.

A Brigade in Line changing Front on a named Company of a named Battalion.

Sec. 16, p. 483. A Brigade in Line changing

Brigadier.	Commanders of Battalions.	Coverers and Supernumerary Serjeants.
Change front on (say) centre of (say) No. 2 Battalion, left thrown forward, the whole in echellon. The Brigadier points out direction. The base Companies are wheeled into the alignment, by Captain of left centre Company (2), (say) six paces. Companies will wheel three paces.	All, "*Change Front on Centre of No. 2 Battalion, Left thrown Forward, the whole in Echellon.*" All, "*Companies will wheel Three Paces.*" Commander of No. 2, "*Right Wing Right about Face, Companies Three Paces Right wheel,*" "*Quick March.*" Commander of No. 1, "*Right about Face, Companies Three Paces Right wheel,*" "*Quick March.*" Commanders of Nos. 3 and 4, "*Companies Three Paces to the Right wheel,*" "*Quick March.*"	Centre Serjeant, on word "Halt" from Captain of left centre Company, steps out, faces to the right, and gives the centre point (1). The two Covering Serjeants of centre Companies give points on outward flank of their Companies facing inwards (1). Coverers of all Companies take up points in succession.
Signal or bugle.	All, "*Quick March.*"	

REMARKS.——"The front rank man of the inner file of the Company that "wheels forward, will be the pivot (3)."

Had the change been made on a flank Company, probably its Supernumerary Serjeant and Coverer would have been placed in position before the wheel of the Company. The same, occasionally, when the change is made on a central Company. When the change is on the two centre Companies, a Supernumerary Serjeant is not required, as the centre Serjeant acts for him, marking the spot on which the change is made.

Part of Field Exercise Book authorizing.——(1) p. 364.   (2) p. 363.

Front on a named Company of a named Battalion.

Brigade Major.	Post of Mounted Regimental Officers.	
	During Movement.	Movement completed.
From the right of left centre Company (the Company thrown forward) dresses its Coverer with the centre Serjeant in a line with the distant point named by the Brigadier. Thus the two base points of the Brigade are settled, and the Brigade Major is enabled to determine on the distant point on the other flank. From the centre of No. 2 dresses the mounted points who come up in succession. Should there be a second Staff Officer, probably each would dress the points of a wing of the Brigade.	Lieutenant-Colonel of No. 2 Battalion near to its centre (6). Lieutenant-Colonels of other Battalions near flank of their Companies which lead in echellon (3). The Senior Major of No. 2 Battalion from the centre, dresses Coverers of both wings of his Battalion (4), assisted by the Serjeant Major. Senior Majors of Nos. 3 and 4, and Junior Major of No. 1, from the rear of the Captain on the flank of their respective leading Companies, see that he leads correctly (3). The Junior Major of No. 2 marks left of his Battalion. They then dress Coverers from outer flank of standing Battalions. Adjutant of No. 2 marks right of his Battalion. Other Adjutants marking the alignment for their respective Battalions.	Commanding Officer (5) 20 paces in rear of centre. Senior Major (5) six paces in rear of right wing. Junior Major (5) six paces in rear of left wing. Adjutant (5) six paces in rear of colours.

On this principle change of front to the right can be made in three ways. On the right flank, by throwing forward the whole of the left. On the left flank, by throwing backward the whole of the right. On any intermediate Company, (indeed, on any file of that Company,) by throwing forward its left, and backward its right. In a similar manner a line can change front to the left in three ways.

(3) Plate XXXIX. (4) No. 7, VI., p. 221. (5) p. 232. (6) Plate XLIII.

No. XXI.

Sec. 16, p. 484.

Brigade in Line changing Front on a named Company of a named Battalion.

Brigadier.	Commanders of Battalions.	Coverers and Supernumerary Serjeants.
Change front on (say) centre of (say) No. 2 Battalion, left thrown forward, remaining Battalions form quarter distance column. The Brigadier points out direction. The base Companies are wheeled into the alignment, by Captain of left centre Company (2), (say) six paces. When quarter distance columns are formed and ready, Signal or bugle.	All, "*Change Front on Centre of No. 2 Battalion, Left thrown forward.*" "*Remaining Battalions, form Quarter distance Column.*" Commander of No. 2, "*Right Wing, Right about Face. Companies Three Paces Right wheel.*" "*Quick March.*" Commander of No. 1, "*Form Quarter Distance Column in Rear of Left Company.*" "*Remaining Companies, Form Fours Left,*" "*Quick March,*" when in column, "*No. 1, Right about Face.*" "*By the Right.*" Commanders of Nos. 3 and 4, "*Form Quarter Distance Column in Rear of Right Company.*" "*Remaining Companies, Form Fours Right,*" "*Quick March.*" All, "*Quick March.*" When in new alignment, all Battalions deploy on their front Companies.	Centre Serjeant, on word "Halt" from Captain of left centre Company, steps out, faces to the right, and gives a centre point (1). The two Covering Serjeants of centre Companies give points on outward flank of their Companies, facing inwards. The other Coverers in succession (1).

REMARKS.——"The front rank man of the inner file of the Company "which wheels forward will be the pivot (1)."

The quarter distance columns are, as a rule, formed in rear of their inner Companies,—but they might be formed in double columns of Companies, or of subdivisions in rear of their centres, should the nature of the ground make such formation desirable (4).

Had the change been made on a flank Company, probably its Supernumerary Serjeant and Coverer would have been placed in position before the wheel of the Company. The same, occasionally, when the change is on a central Company.

Part of Field Exercise Book authorizing.——(1) p. 364.   (2) p. 363.

Line changing Front on a named Company of Battalion.

Brigade Major.	Post of Mounted Regimental Officers.	
	During Movement.	Movement completed.
From the right of the left centre Company (the Company thrown forward) dresses its Coverer (with the centre Serjeant) in a line with the distant point named by the Brigadier. Thus the two base points of the Brigade are settled, and the Brigade Major is enabled to determine upon the distant point, on the other flank. From the centre of No. 2 he dresses the mounted points who come up successively. If there is a second Staff Officer, probably each would dress the points of a wing of the Brigade.	Lieutenant-Colonel of No. 2 near to its centre (5). Lieutenant-Colonels of Battalions in quarter distance columns on inner flank, aligning with leading Company. The Senior Major (2) of No 2 Battalion dresses Coverers of both wings of his Battalion, assisted by Serjeant Major. Junior Major of No. 2 marks left of his Battalion. Each Senior Major of 1, 3, and 4 keeping "his own face in line with the loading rank of the column" (7), "superintends the direction" so as to lead it within six paces of the Adjutant of the preceding Battalion. Deploying, Senior Majors of 3 and 4, Junior of No. 1, see to dressing of Coverers. Junior Majors of Nos. 1, 3, and 4, in the rear of pivots, attending to covering of Officers (6). Adjutant of No. 2 marks right of his Battalion. Other Adjutants mark in the alignment deploying distance and six paces for their respective Battalions.	Each Commanding Officer 20 paces in rear of centre (3). Each Senior Major six paces in rear of centre of right wing (3). Each Junior Major six paces in rear of centre of left wing (3). Each Adjutant six paces in rear of colours (3).

When the change is made on the two centre Companies, a Supernumerary Serjeant is not required, because the centre Serjeant acts for him, marking the spot on which the change is made.

On this principle, change of front to the right can be made in three ways. On the right flank, by throwing forward the whole of the left. On the left flank, by throwing backward the whole of the right. On any intermediate Company, (indeed, on any file of that Company,) by throwing forward its left, and backward its right. In a similar manner a line can change front to the left in three ways.

(3) p. 232.   (4) Plate LIX.   (5) Plate XLIII.   (6) p. 225.   (7) 14, p. 451.

No. XXII.

Sec. 17, p. 487.

A Brigade from Line changing Position on Detached Points.

Sec. 17, p. 487. A Brigade from Line

Brigadier.	Commanders of Battalions.	Coverers and Supernumerary Serjeants.
Change position to the (say) right on detached points. Battalions will form quarter distance columns in rear of their right Companies. Gives general direction of future position. On completion of columns, Signal or bugle. Or the command might be, "Battalions will form quarter distance (7) double column of subdivisions in rear of their centre."	All, " *Change Position to the Right on Detached Points. Battalions will form Quarter Distance Columns in Rear of their Right Companies.*" All, "*No. — Quarter Distance Column in Rear of No. 1 Company,*" "*Remainder, Form Fours Right,*" "*Quick March*" (1). All, "*Quick March.*" N.B.—Battalions move by the shortest lines to the point of entry, deploy as they arrive on new alignment, or wait for Brigadier's command, as may be ordered.	Supernumerary Serjeant of front Company of No. 1 facing to the right marks the point of appui, placing himself in line with the head of the Major's horse (5). Its Coverer takes the Company's distance from him. The Supernumerary Serjeants of the other leading Companies of each Battalion (accompanied by Coverers) will run out when 20 paces from the new alignment, and take up points in it at six paces from the mounted point who is marking the outer flank of the Battalion already in the alignment (5).

REMARKS.——As the point of appui is on the right, all Battalions march by the right, therefore unless there is a reason for the contrary, form column in rear of their right Companies.

If Battalions come up in double column of subdivisions, the Senior Majors must lead their columns into the new alignment at wing distance and six paces from the Adjutant of the Battalion which precedes theirs.

Part of Field Exercise Book authorizing.——(1) p. 294.   (2) p. 250.
(7) Quarter distance, see Plate LIX.

changing Position on Detached Points.

Brigade Major.	Post of Mounted Regimental Officers.	
	During Movement.	Movement completed.
Places himself at the point of appui (tho point of entry in the new alignment). Selects a distant point in the direction named by the Brigadier, and places the Senior Major of the Right Battalion at the point of appui. From, say 30 paces, without the point of appui, dresses its Adjutant in a line with the Major and the distant point. The Brigade Major will find that by placing himself outside the Major in a line with the Major and distant point, that the Adjutant is much assisted in getting into the alignment. Had he a spare mounted point, of course he would prefer placing him there (8). The other Adjutants are dressed in succession.	Lieutenant-Colonels on the left (the proper pivot flank) of their leading Companies, while in quarter distance column (3). Senior Major of No. 1 at first on the right (the inner flank), near Lieutenant of leading Company, "to superintend the direction" (3 and 9); approaching the alignment, he marks the Brigade point of appui (5). Junior Major of No. 1 then comes up and keeping "his own face in line with the leading rank of the column," leads it (by the right) to the point of appui (6). Other Senior Majors on the inner flank (the right) lead in a similar manner their respective columns to within six paces of the Adjutant of the preceding Battalion. Deploying, see to dressing of Coverers from the right. Junior Majors (9) of 2, 3, and 4 from the rear see to covering of Officers (2). Adjutants (3) two paces from reverse flank of right centre Company. Successively mark the deploying distance of their Battalions in the new alignment.	After deployment, Commanding Officers (4) 20 paces in rear of centre. Senior Major (4) six paces in rear of centre of right wing. Junior Major (4) six paces in rear of centre of left wing. Adjutants (4) six paces in rear of colours.

The Adjutants take distance for left wings.

"When thought expedient, the Battalions may move off at once in open "column from the flanks or centre, and close to quarter distance on the "march."

(3) pp. 225, 250.   (4) p. 232.   (5) Nos. 3 & 5, p. 448.   (6 14, p. 451.
  (8) 2, p. 220.   (9) note, p. 63, this book.

No. XXIII.

Sec. 17, p. 487.

A Brigade from Line changing Position on Detached Points.

Sec. 17, p. 487. A Brigade from Line

Brigadier.	Commanders of Battalions.	Coverers and Supernumerary Serjeants.
Change position to the (say) right on detached points. Advance in fours from the right of Companies. Signal or bugle.	All, " *Change Position to the Right on Detached Points. Advance in Fours from the Right of Companies.*" All, "*Form Fours Right,*" "*By the Right.*" Captains on *right* (1). All, " *Quick March.*" The Companies form in open column on their Coverers, and are then wheeled into line by Companies or Battalions in succession — or the whole Brigade may be wheeled into line at one time, as may be ordered.	Supernumerary of front Company of No. 1 facing to the right marks the point of appui, placing himself in line with the head of the Major's horse (2). All its Coverers run out in succession when 20 paces from new alignment (4), face to the right, (the point of appui,) and take up distance for their respective Companies, and when covered, face to the right about (6). The Supernumerary Serjeants of the other leading Companies of each Battalion run out when 20 paces from the new alignment, and take up points in it at six paces from the mounted point who is marking the outer flank of the Battalion already in the alignment (3).

REMARKS.——The new line is generally formed on a flank Battalion. As in the present instance the named change is to the right, the point of appui (in the new line) will be on the right; therefore, the dressing must be from the right, Companies must advance in fours from the right, the Captains must be on the right of their fours (1) and preserve distance, not for their own, but for the next Companies on their right (6).

Coming near the alignment, No. 1 Company marches on its Supernumerary

Part of Field Exercise Book authorizing.——(1) p. 274.   (2) V., p. 220.
(7) p. 232.

changing Position on Detached Points.

Brigade Major.	Post of Mounted Regimental Officers.	
	During Movement.	Movement completed.
Places himself at the point of appui (the point of entry in the new alignment). Selects a distant point in the direction named by the Brigadier, places the Senior Major of the right Battalion at the point of appui. From, say 30 paces, without the point of appui, dresses its Adjutant in a line with the Major and the distant point. The Brigade Major will find that by placing himself in a line with the Major and the distant point, the Adjutant is much assisted in getting into the alignment. Had he a spare mounted point, of course he would prefer placing him there (8). The other Adjutants are dressed in succession.	Lieutenant-Colonels in rear of central Companies watching movement, or on inner flank. Senior Majors on inner flank, (the right,) attending to the direction taken by Captain who leads No. 1 Company, and to the aligning of the heads of Companies (5). Junior Majors near centre of their left wings (5). Adjutants in rear of centre of their Battalions (5).	Commanding Officer (7) 20 paces in rear of centre. Senior Major (7) six paces in rear of right wing. Junior Major (7) six paces in rear of left wing. Adjutant (7) six paces in rear of colours.

Serjeant; the remaining not on their own, but on the Coverer of the Companies respectively preceding them in column (6).

It would be wrong to advance in fours from the left of Companies, as in such case the right Company of the right Battalion marching on the point of appui, would not have room to wheel into line.

Each Battalion in a Brigade may be ordered to move in a different formation, according to the nature of the ground.

(3) 5, p. 449.   (4) V., p. 230.   (5) p. 225.   (6) Plate LX., p. 295.
(8) 2, p. 220.

No. XXIV.

Sec. 18, p. 488.

A Brigade in Line of Contiguous Columns, at Close or Quarter Distance, deploying into Line.

Sec. 18, p. 488. *A Brigade in Line of Contiguous into*

Brigadier.	Commanders of Battalions.	Coverers and Supernumerary Serjeants.
The Brigade will deploy on (say) No. 3 Company of (say) No. 2 Battalion. Signal or bugle.	All, "*The Brigade will deploy on No. 3 Company of No. 2 Battalion.*" Commander of No. 2, "*Deploy on No. 3 Company. Remaining Companies Form Fours outwards*" (1). Commander of No. 1, "*Form Fours Right,*" "*By the Left.*" Commanders of Nos. 3 and 4, "*Form Fours Left,*" "*By the Right.*" All, "*Quick March.*" The inner flank Company of each of the Battalions which moves to a flank is halted by its Lieutenant-Colonel; remaining Companies by their respective Captains.	Coverer and Supernumerary of No. 3 Company of No. 2 Battalion run out to front and give base points, facing inwards; Coverer on reverse, Supernumerary on pivot flank (3), being covered in line with the heads of the mounted points (6). Other Coverers come out when their Companies get within 20 paces of their respective points of formation, and return to their places, on second Company, from them receiving word, "Eyes front" (2).

REMARKS.——Should an advance be required in line of close or quarter distance columns, at deploying distance, (sec. 9, p. 474,) before deploying into line, the contiguous columns could be opened out to deploying distance from any (say a central) Battalion. Points would be taken up in the same manner as when a Brigade changes position on detached points, see page 106 this book.

For orders regarding the advance of quarter distance columns at deploying distance, see page 62 this book.

For orders regarding the advance of double columns of subdivisions, see remarks, page 135.

Part of Field Exercise Book authorizing.——(1) p. 323.   (2) V., p. 230.
(6) V., p. 220.

Columns, at Close or Quarter Distance, deploying Line.

Brigade Major.	Post of Mounted Regimental Officers.	
	During Movement.	Movement completed.
From the left flank of third Company of No. 2 Battalion (the point of appui) on its Senior Major dresses its Junior Major or its Adjutant, as case may be, in the direction named by the Brigadier. On these two mounted points, the third mounted point of No. 2 covers, in the opposite direction. The Brigade Major then dresses the Adjutants of the other Battalions.	Senior Major of No. 2 Battalion, with his horse's head at arm's length, from the left flank of front Company of No. 2 marks the point of appui, and afterwards dresses Coverers (1). Its Junior Major marks the left of the Battalion, its Adjutant the right. The other Senior Majors see that their Companies are led properly. Other Junior Majors see that leaders of Companies cover exactly, or relatively (as case may be) (7). Junior Major of No. 1, and Senior Majors of Nos. 3 and 4, dress Coverers (4).	Commanding Officer (5) 20 paces in rear of centre. Senior Major (5) six paces in rear of right wing. Junior Major (5) six paces in rear of left wing. Adjutant (5) six paces in rear of colours.

A Brigade in contiguous columns may deploy on any named Company of any named Battalion.

A Brigade in mass may deploy on any named Company of any named Battalion without previously forming line of contiguous columns; the named Battalion would move up to the front base and deploy as usual; the remaining Battalions would move by the shortest lines to the points where their inner flanks ought to rest, and then deploy.

(3) p. 323, plate XXXVI.   (4) No. 7, p. 220.   (5) p. 232.
(7) p. 461.

No. XXV.

Sec. 19, p. 491.

A Brigade in Mass of Battalion Columns opening out to Deploying Distance on Detached Points, and deploying into Line.

Sec. 19, *p.* 491. *A Brigade in Mass of Battalion Detached Points, and*

Brigadier.	Commanders of Battalions.	Coverers and Supernumerary Serjeants.
The Brigade will deploy into line of columns at deploying distance on detached points. Rear columns disengage to the (say) left by fours. Signal or bugle. The Battalions may be ordered to deploy into line in succession as they come up, or simultaneously after the line of columns is completed.	All "*The Brigade will deploy into Line of Columns at Deploying Distance on Detached Points. Rear Columns disengage to the Left by Fours.*" Commander of leading Battalion, "*No. —— will Advance,*" "*By the Right.*" Lieutenants leading. Commanders of other Battalions, "*Form Fours Left,*" "*By the Right.*" All "*Quick March,*" and lead their Battalions to the point of entry by the shortest lines,—bringing them up parallel to the new alignment,—halting them,—and, if necessary, dressing them.	Supernumeraries and Coverers of leading Companies run out (1) when 20 paces from the alignment. Supernumerary Serjeant of front Company of No. 1 gives a point close to and in line with the head of the Major's horse—Covering Serjeant at Company distance from him. The Supernumeraries take up points at six paces from the Adjutants of the Regiments on the right. Coverers at Companies' distance from Supernumeraries.

REMARKS.——Were the Battalions in double column of subdivisions, as the Senior Major of No. 1 must mark the point of appui and the Adjutant deploying distance, it is clear that the Junior Major ought to lead the column, so that its centre shall be half way between the said points (3). The other Battalions would be led in a similar manner by their respective Senior Majors (3).

Part of Field Exercise Book authorizing.——(1) No. V., p. 230.   (2) pp. 225, 250.

Columns opening out to Deploying Distance on deploying into Line.

Brigade Major.	Post of Mounted Regimental Officers.	
	During Movement.	Movement completed.
From the right, the point of formation (or appui),* determines on a distant point in the direction named by the Brigadier, and places the Senior Major of No. 1 at the point of appui—and as a guide to its Adjutant probably places himself about 30 paces outside the point of appui in a line with the Senior Major and the distant point —or, should he have an available mounted point he can place it there (4). He dresses the Adjutants as they come up in succession. * The Brigadier's order for the rear columns to disengage to the left shows that the point of appui must be on the right.	Lieutenant-Colonels on the left (the pivot flank) of their leading Companies (2). Senior Major of No. 1 places himself at the point of appui. Senior Majors of other Battalions on the right, (the inner flank,) near Lieutenants of leading Companies, "to superintend the direction" (2). Deploying, dress Coverers from the right. Junior Majors (6) superintending covering of Officers from rear (2). Adjutant of No. 1 takes deploying distance on the alignment — other Adjutants their deploying distance and six paces.	Commanding Officers 20 paces in rear of centre (5). Senior Major six paces in rear of right wing (5). Junior Major six paces in rear of left wing (5). Adjutant six paces in rear of colours (5).

Plate LXI. shows how little an inversion is regarded, for right in front is usually represented in the plates; therefore, in the new position there represented, the order of the Brigade is inverted as it stands in line. All the Battalions would deploy on their rear Companies.

(3) Plate LX.   (4) 2, p. 220.   (5) p. 232.   (6) note, p. 63, this book.

No. XXVI.

Sec. 20, p. 492.

Brigade advancing from Line by the Flank March of Fours.

Sec. 20, p. 492. *A Brigade advancing from*

Brigadier.	Commanders of Battalions.	Coverers and Supernumerary Serjeants.
The Brigade will advance in fours from the (say) right of Companies. No. (say) 3 Company of No. (say) 2 Battalion will regulate.	All, "*The Brigade will advance in Fours from the Right of Companies. No. 3 Company of No. 2 Battalion will regulate.*" All,"*Form Fours Right,*" "*Left wheel.*" Commander of No. 2 Battalion, "*By No. 3 Company.*" Commander of No. 1, "*By the Left.*" Commanders of Nos. 3 and 4, "*By the Right.*" Captains *shifting to inner flank* (2).	Coverers to head of the front rank of fours (4).
Signal or bugle. At any moment, "*The Brigade will form Line to the Front.*"	All, "*Quick March.*"	
Signal or bugle.	All repeat, "*The Brigade will form Line to the Front.*" All, "*Front form Line.*"	
Or, previous to forming line, the Brigade will form Battalion squares on (say) right centre Companies.*	All, "*The Brigade will form Battalion Squares on Right Centre Companies.*"	
Signal or bugle. * The columns should wheel ¼ of a circle to avoid firing into one another.	All, No. — "*On Right Centre Company Form Square — Wings Inwards turn.*"	

Part of Field Exercise Book authorizing.——(1) 225.   (2) 274.   (3) p. 282.

Line by the Flank March of Fours. 123

Brigade Major.	Post of Mounted Regimental Officers.	
	During Movement.	Movement completed.
From left of the right section of fours of No. 3 Company of No. 2 Battalion, names distant point for Captain to march on — and has a general superintendence over the dressing of the Coverers (5). On any Battalion closing to quarter distance, (or to close column,) sees to dressing of its mounted Officers, who are marking the full distance.	Each Lieutenant-Colonel (1) in rear, near centre of his Battalion. Senior Major of No. 2 on left flank of No. 3 Company, looking to march of leader of No. 3 Company on distant point, and assists Brigade Major in dressing heads of Companies. Senior Majors (6) of Nos. 3 and 4 on inner (the right) flank, looking to march of leader of inner Company, and to dressing of heads of Companies. Junior Major (6) of No. 1 the same, from left (his inner flank). Other Junior Majors (1), in rear near centre of their own wings. Adjutants (1) in rear, near centre of their Battalions.	Lieutenant-Colonel (1) in rear, near centre of his Battalion. Senior Major (1) of No. 2 on left flank of No. 3 Company. Senior Majors (1) of Nos. 3 and 4 on inner (the right) flank. Junior Major (1) of No. 1 on left (his inner) flank. Other Junior Majors (1) in rear, near centre of their own wings. Adjutants (1) in rear, near centre of their own Battalions.

(4) Sec. 20, p. 97.   (5) Sec. 25, p. 275.   (6) End of No. 1, IV., p. 219.

[*For Remarks see over.*

REMARKS.——" The Battalion (and" Company of that "Battalion) which " is the least likely to be interrupted by obstacles, will be selected to direct."

" The direction of the advance may be changed by" gradually "altering " direction of the regulating Company. The remaining Companies and Battalions " conforming."

Leaders of Companies to the right of regulating Company are on the left (the inner) flank (2), preserving distance for their own Companies.

Leaders of Companies to the left of regulating Company are on the right flank, preserving distance for the Company next to them on the right.

The leader of the innermost Company of all Battalions, excepting the regulating one, is answerable for Company's distance plus six paces, in the same manner that he would be answerable were the Brigade to be suddenly moved to a flank, and thereby become a column advancing or retiring (3).

No. XXVII.

Sec. 21, p. 493.

A Brigade from Line forming Square.

Sec. 21, p. 493.   A Brigade

Brigadier.	Commanders of Battalions.	Coverers and Supernumerary Serjeants.
The Battalions will form quarter distance column (say) right in front on (say) right centre Companies. Signal or bugle. Direct echellon of Battalions from (say) No. 2, at (say) 200 paces' distance (3), and form squares. Nos. 3 and 4 will retire. Signal or bugle.	All, "*Battalions will form Quarter Distance Column Right in Front on Right Centre Companies.*" All, "*Form Fours inwards.*" All, *Quick March.*" All, "*Direct Echellon of Battalions from No. 2 at 200 paces' distance, and form Squares.*" "*Nos. 3 and 4 will retire.*" Commander of No. 1, "*No 1 will advance.*" "*By the Left.*" Commanders of Nos. 3 and 4, "*Right about Face.*" "*By the Left.*" All, (excepting Commander of No. 2,) "*Quick March,*" and subsequently all "*Form Square.*" Or each Battalion might form square as soon as it takes up its distance in echellon.	Every Coverer of a right centre Company marks in front where next Company will rest (1). He covers on his Captain and faces about Other Coverers of right wings act on same principle (1). Coverers of left wing give points for their own Companies (1).
Or, (without forming in echellon,) while in quarter distance column, " the "Battalions will wheel "four paces to the (say) "left," — or the wheel might be done by the eye, when the order would be for the Battalions to wheel ¼ of a circle.	All, "*The Battalions will wheel Four Paces to the Left.*" All, "*No. — Four Paces to the Left wheel,*" (2) or the wheel might be done by the eye, which would be better.	Coverer of leading Companies steps four paces from the 8th file, if done methodically* (4). * Useful as a drill — but impracticable on service.

Part of Field Exercise Book authorizing.——(1) p. 297.   (2) p. 454.
(6) p. 296.   (7) pp. 250 and 225.   (8) Note, p. 63 this book.

from Line forming Square. 127

Brigade Major.	Post of Mounted Regimental Officers.	
	During Movement.	Movement completed.
Dresses no points.	Lieutenant-Colonel from near the centre watches the formation. Senior Major superintends the covering from the front (1). Junior Major and Adjutant after assisting during manœuvre move to the places they will occupy in quarter distance column (6).	Lieutenant-Colonel on pivot flank of leading Company (7). Senior Major two paces from reverse flank of centre of right wing (7). Junior Major two paces from reverse flank of centre of left wing (7). Adjutant two paces from reverse flank of right centre Company (7).
Dresses no points.	Lieutenant-Colonels on the proper left flank. The Senior Majors superintend covering from proper front when halted (1). The Junior Major of No. 1, the Seniors of Nos. 3 and 4, see to covering of Officers on the move (8). Adjutants on centre of reverse flank (7).	All inside square.
Dresses no points.	Lieutenant-Colonel near pivot (on left) (5). Senior Major reverse flank of right wing (5). Junior Major from rear on reverse flank looks to covering of Lieutenants (5). Adjutants on reverse flank near centre (5).	Same as above.

(3) "at least half their front," p. 453.   (4) p. 261.   (5) Plate XXVII. iv. p. 219.
[*For Remarks see over.*

REMARKS.—Brigade squares, or squares consisting of several Battalions, can seldom be necessary, although they may be formed from columns, on the same principle as a Battalion square. If from double columns of Companies, subdivisions will wheel outwards, to form the side faces instead of sections.

Battalion squares flanking each other, in direct echellon, afford the readiest and most efficient defence. When time will admit, the Battalions of a Brigade in Line should be advanced in direct echellon to any required distance before forming squares.

Were there an advance in direct echellon, the leading Battalion would direct without its being necessary to give any caution to that effect (2). Distance, therefore, would be preserved from the right. All would be conducted on the principle laid down in Sec. 9, p. 63 this book. The Adjutant of No. 2 would follow in a line six paces clear of the Junior Major of No. 1. The Adjutant of No. 3 would follow in a line six paces clear of the Junior Major of No. 2.

No. XXVIII.

Sec. 23, p. 497.

Two Lines changing Front on the Flank of the First Line.

Sec. 23, p. 497. Two Lines changing Front on the second, a Line of Quarter Distance

Brigadier.	Commanders of Battalions.	Coverers and Supernumerary Serjeants.
Of First Line. Change front upon the right flank of the first line, left thrown forward.	*Of First Line.* All, " *Change Front upon the Right Flank of the First Line, Left thrown Forward.*" The first line proceeds to change its front as in Sec. 16, p. 98 of this book.	
Of Second Line. The second line will change position on detached points in rear of the first line. Signal or bugle.	*Of Second Line.* All, " *The Second Line will change Position upon Detached Points, in Rear of the First Line.*" Commander of No. 1 Battalion of second line, (probably) " *Fours Left.*" Commanders of other Battalions (probably) " *Advance by the Right.*" Lieutenants lead. In short, all move by the shortest line to their respective points. All, " *Quick March.*"	*Of Second Line.* Supernumerary Serjeants and Coverers of the leading Companies of all the columns in second line take up points for breadth of their respective columns in a line with horses' heads of mounted points (1). They run out when 20 paces from their positions in the new alignment.

Part of Field Exercise Book authorizing.——(1) V. p. 220. (2) Plates LXII.

REMARKS.——The second line has its point of appui and its directing Battalion exactly the same as has the first line.

The point of appui in the second line is directly in rear of the point of appui in the first line. In general the distance should be equal to the front of two Battalions. The distance between lines should be sufficient to prevent any liability to disorder by the unforeseen retreat of the first line.

In the present instance the columns moved into the new position by the right, because the point of appui was on the right.

Flank of the First Line. (The first is a Line deployed, Columns at Deploying Distance.)

Brigade Major.	Post of Mounted Regimental Officers.	
	During Movement.	Movement completed.
Of Second Line. Places a point at the required distance (say equal to the frontage of two Battalions,) directly in rear of the right, the point of appui of first line. This constitutes the point of appui (the point of entry) of second line.—A point of direction may also be given passing through it in prolongation of the line, which should be parallel to the front line (4). He may select a distant point on which to dress the line.	*Of Second Line.* Lieutenant-Colonels each on the proper flank near his leading Company. Senior Majors on the right (the inner) flank near leaders of leading Companies, "to superintend the direction" (3). Junior Majors on outer flank attend to covering of Officers (5). If the point of appui be marked by a foot-point, the Major of No. 1 replaces him. Adjutants move out to mark the alignment at deploying distance for their respective Battalions.	*Of Second Line.* Lieutenant-Colonels (4) on proper pivot flank, aligning with leading Companies. Senior Majors (3) on reverse flank, two paces from centre of right wings. Junior Majors (3) on reverse flank, two paces from centre of left wings. Adjutants (3) on reverse flank, two paces from right centre Companies.

and LXIII.   (3) pp. 250, 225.   (4) 2, p. 220.   (5) Note, p. 63, this book.

Second lines are usually composed of single or double quarter distance columns of Battalions at deploying distance.

They are regulated by the column which is in rear of the directing Battalion in the first line. Generally speaking (see p. 492) if that column be single and right in front, it will be in rear of the right Company of the regulating Battalion of front line. If that column be single and left in front, it will be in rear of the left Company. If that column be double, it will be in rear of the centre of the "Battalion (2) of direction" in the first line.

[*Remarks continued on p.* 132.

This covering is regulated on the general principle that when the column is deployed, it will, as far as is practicable, cover the Battalion of direction.

The remaining columns of the second line will keep deploying distance from the regulating Battalion.

See observations at foot of page 134 of this book.

The movements of the second line must correspond with those of the first. If the first line makes a change of front, the second line must make a corresponding change, (forming parallel to it) on a point placed perpendicularly in rear of the point of appui of the first line.

When the second line is required to relieve the first, it will be deployed and advance. When it approaches within the strongest Company's wheeling distance of the first line, the first line having received its Brigadier's word, to the effect that the Brigade will From the Right of Companies pass by Fours to the Rear, and the word from the Commanders "Form Fours Right," "Right Wheel;" on signal, "Quick March," it will proceed to the rear through the second line (245), (which will throw back the necessary files.) It will close to quarter distance on the march on any named Company (p. 133),—turn to the front, and its Battalions will wheel the quarter circle, forming a line of quarter distance columns at deploying distance, parallel with the new front line.

"Reserves should, as far as is practicable, be kept under cover and protected "from the enemy's artillery." It should too be borne in mind that at long ranges a quarter distance column is more likely to be injured by an enemy's fire than is a close column. This is fully explained in the "Regulations for Musketry Instruction," page 27.

It may be asked,—if the first line changes front to the left on the left flank, how is the "Battalion of direction" in the second line (composed of quarter distance single columns right in front,) to obey the order to be " in rear of the right "Company of the Battalion of direction of the first line," and yet "form" "on a "point placed perpendicularly in rear of the point of appui of the first line?" Plate LXI. answers the question. It clearly shows, that the latter is considered the more important object of the two. It represents a Brigade of quarter distance columns right in front taking up a line at deploying distance on detached points from the left; the Plate shows that such columns move by the left—come into position by the left—and if ordered to deploy, would do so on their *rear* Companies.

No. XXIX.

Sec. 24, p. 498.

Two Lines changing Front upon a Central Point of the First Line.

134   Sec. 24, p. 498. *Two Lines changing Front upon a deployed, the second is a Line of Quarter*

Brigadier.	Commanders of Battalions.	Coverers and Supernumerary Serjeants.
Of First Line. Change front upon the centre of (say) No. 2 of the first line, (say) right thrown back.	All repeat Brigadier's word. Commanders of Battalions in front line proceed as described in Sec. 16, pages 98 and 102 of this book.	
Of Second Line. The second line will change position on detached points in rear of the first line, suppose single columns at quarter distance, right in front. Signal or bugle.	All Commanders of Battalions in second line (probably) give the order, " *Form Fours Left*," " *By the Right.*" In short, all move by the shortest line to their respective points. All, " *Quick March.*"	*Of Second Line.* Supernumerary and Coverer of leading Company of every column of second line, when 20 paces from alignment, run out to give points for their respective columns, aligning with the horses' heads of mounted points (7).

Part of Field Exercise Book authorizing.——(1) p. 250, and end of No. 1, IV., (6) 2, p. 220.   (7) V., p. 220.

REMARKS.——See remarks in page 131.

As the change is made on the centre of No. 2 of the first line, No. 2 in the second line must become its directing Battalion. The regulating Battalion will form on its Senior Major (placed at the point of appui). Its Junior Major marks left wing distance. Its Adjutant right wing distance. No. 1 Battalion forms at deploying distance and six paces from Adjutant of No. 2. No. 3 comes

Central Point of the First Line. (The first is a Line 135
Distance Columns at Deploying Distance.)

Brigade Major.	Post of Mounted Regimental Officers.	
	During Movement.	Movement completed.
Of Second Line. From a point* probably given by Staff Officer in rear of the central point (the point of appui) in first line, (at a distance equal to about the front of two Battalions in a line perpendicular to the first line,) selects distant points on both flanks, or places them parallel to the first line. If he require it he may place a point of direction (6).	*Of Second Line.* Nearly in the same position they were before their quarter distance columns were faced to the left in fours. Lieutenant - Colonels each on inner flank. Senior Majors (1) on the right, superintending direction. Junior Majors on outer flank, attending to covering of Officers (8). Adjutants near centre in rear (1).	*Of Second Line.* Lieutenant - Colonels (4) on proper pivot flank, aligning with leading Company. Senior Majors (4) on proper reverse flank, two paces from centre of their right wings. Junior Majors (4) on reverse flank, two paces from centre of their left wings. Adjutants (4) on reverse flank, two paces from right centre Company.
* Which point is the point of appui of second line.		

p. 219. (2) p. 487. (3) Plate LXIII. (4) pp. 225, 250. (5) Sec. 9, No. 1, p. 474. (8) Note, p. 63, this book.

into the alignment at six paces from Junior Major of No. 2. No. 4 comes into the alignment at six paces from Adjutant of No. 3. (2.)

Double Columns.

When the second line is composed of double columns of subdivisions, those Junior Majors who are on the right of the regulating column lead their respective double

[*Remarks continued on p.* 136.

columns to wing distance and six paces from the Adjutant of Battalion on their left. The Senior Majors who are on the left of the regulating Battalion lead their respective double columns to wing distance and six paces from Adjutants* of Battalions on their right (3).

Should the two lines advance, the regulating column and the columns on its left will be directed by the Senior Majors—the columns on the right of the regulating columns by the Junior Majors. Those Officers (5) place themselves on the inner flank of their respective leading subdivisions, and direct the march of their columns so as to keep the deploying distances of their inner wings and six paces from the Adjutants* of the Battalions next to them.

---

* The wing distance of the Battalion next to and on the left of the regulating Battalion is kept from the Junior Major of the regulating Battalion.

Advances and Retreats.

"The advance and retreat of alternate bodies are per-
"formed in a line composed of a large body of troops, either
"by brigades, battalions, or half battalions, according to
"the principle laid down for the battalion in Part IV., S. 8.

"When the retreat is by battalions or brigades, the
"distance they retire alternately beyond each other must
"depend on circumstances, but in order to afford mutual
"protection and support, and to ensure a continued and
"steady resistance to the enemy, it should rarely exceed
"two hundred yards. In retiring, one body will protect
"the retreat of another; and when the enemy presses hard,
"the retreating or rear line will turn to the front and form
"in the intervals of the first; the whole being supported by
"the reserve." (p. 455.)

"The intervals left in the front line by the bodies which
"have retreated will be occupied by light infantry. Each
"part of the line will move by a directing Battalion, or
"half Battalion, and any faults in either part of the line
"when halted should be corrected before the other part
"reaches it. The retiring part of the line will march
"direct upon the intervals between the battalions or half
"battalions in its rear, and when it has passed them it will
"move by its directing body." (p. 455.)

Echellons, Direct and Oblique.

"Echellon formations and movements are conducted in
"a line composed of a large body of troops, upon the prin-

" ciples laid down in Part IV. They are calculated to place
" a body of troops in an advantageous position to gain an
" enemy's flank ; and sometimes they are formed with effect
" from the centre of a line, by refusing each wing. If an
" attack made by an advanced corps of a great echellon be
" effectual, each succeeding one moves up to improve the
" advantage ; if it fails, the succeeding bodies are in a situa-
" tion to protect the retreat ; and in gradually retiring upon
" each other, they afford mutual aid and support." (p. 453.)

" A direct echellon, composed of a large body of troops,
" is formed by the successive advance of brigades or batta-
" lions from either flank, or from the centre of a line, or by
" columns placed in echellon parallel to the enemy's position;
" and in both cases, the distance of at least half their front
" will be preserved between the several parts of the echellon,
" in order to give sufficient room for the mutual protection
" of flanking squares, when such formation is required."
(p. 453.)

" A line is thrown into oblique echellon for the pur-
" pose of gaining ground to a flank; in large bodies of
" troops the oblique echellon should be composed of com-
" panies (vide S. 53, Part IV.), as deviating least from the
" line formation, which can at any moment be resumed by
" halting and wheeling the companies back upon their
" pivots, (vide S. 54, Part IV.) These echellons at a dis-
" tance have the appearance of a complete line ; by this means
" a flank movement may be made almost imperceptibly to an
" enemy." (p. 453.)

" When the object is to gain an enemy's flank, the
" whole line will be thrown into echellon towards that flank
" of the enemy which it is intended to attack or turn ; care
" being taken in such advances that the outer flanks of the
" echellon are protected from the enfilade of the enemy.
" When it is necessary to refuse a flank attacked by an

" enemy, the line will be partially thrown into echellon from
" that flank direct to the rear; but when the enemy's attack
" is repulsed, a counter attack may be made upon him with
" advantage, by an advance in echellon from the other flank."
(pp. 453, 454.)

" When the flank of a line is refused in this manner
" by a partial retreat in echellon of battalions, the flank
" that remains halted should (if possible) be posted upon a
" strong position, from which the fire of artillery could
" enfilade the advancing enemy." (p. 454.)

" In an open country, where the enemy is in a position
" whence he can observe their intention, echellon movements
" to attack or gain a flank are attended with difficulty and
" risk; advantage must therefore be taken of any objects, or
" ground, that may afford the means of partial concealment."
(p. 454.)

" Wings of battalions, companies, or parts of com-
" panies in echellon will move by their directing flanks, as
" explained in Part IV.; columns in echellon will also move
" by their flanks on similar principles; but battalions in
" line moving in echellon of battalions will march by their
" centres, the leading battalion of the echellon being in-
" variably the battalion of direction." (p. 454.)

" Oblique and direct echellons may be formed of quarter
" distance columns. Direct echellons, whether of lines or
" columns, may be composed of small or large bodies moving
" in concert, according to circumstances and the object con-
" templated; the chief precaution to be observed, is that the
" different parts of the echellon are never so far separated as
" to prevent their mutually supporting each other." (p. 454.)

" It may be assumed as a principle, that great echellon
" movements, preparatory to action, and previous to coming
" under the fire of artillery, will be made in quarter-distance
" columns; and that echellon movements of the line, when

" under fire, will be made either in oblique echellon of com-
" panies, or in direct echellon of battalions or larger bodies."
(p. 454.)

" The attacks of armies are generally conducted on the
" principles of the echellon. There are few situations where
" the whole could act at the same time, or where it would be
" desirable or prudent that they should do so." (p. 455.)

Inversions and Changes of Front.

" Great celerity may frequently be given to the move-
" ments of extensive bodies by battalions changing front
" individually on their own ground, so as to invert the order
" of a brigade or division. This inversion can never be
" attended with any embarrassment or confusion, as the order
" in which the battalions of a brigade are arranged is a
" matter of no importance. A change of front to the rear
" can by this means be accomplished in a line of contiguous
" columns, by the countermarch of each battalion on its own
" ground." (pp. 455, 456.)

Movements to be Covered by Light Infantry.

" All movements in line and changes of front or position
" in presence of an enemy should be protected by light
" infantry; the distance between the line and the skirmishers
" must depend on the nature of the ground and the character
" of the movement. When a line is advancing, and still far
" distant from the enemy, the skirmishers should be at a
" considerable distance in front, with supports and reserves;

" as the line approaches the enemy, the distance of the
" skirmishers must be reduced, and the line itself will be a
" sufficient reserve, the skirmishers and supports only re-
" maining in front. When near the enemy, skirmishers may
" occasionally be used with advantage close in front of the
" line, without supports; they may be directed to lie down
" while the battalions fire over them, and then to run on to
" cover the further advance, or run to the rear through the
" intervals between battalions." (p. 456.)

Reserves.

" When a body of troops is formed with a view to
" attacking or resisting an enemy, a portion of it should
" always be kept in reserve. The reserve may be concen-
" trated in one place, or divided, as circumstances may re-
" quire. Troops in reserve should generally remain in
" column, as in that formation they can readily be moved
" to any point where their services are required. Reserves
" should, as far as practicable, be kept under cover and
" protected from the enemy's artillery." (p. 446.)

" Large bodies of troops in reserve may, at the discre-
" tion of the general commanding, be ordered to unfix
" bayonets." (p. 456.)

Position of Artillery.

Section 25, p. 498. Position of a Battery of Artillery when moving with a Brigade.

" The usual position of a battery of artillery, when in
" line, is on the right, with an interval of $22\frac{1}{2}$ yards, $28\frac{1}{2}$
" yards, or $34\frac{1}{2}$ yards, according to the number of horses in
" the guns, whether four, six, or eight.

" When the battalions are in contiguous quarter-distance
" columns, the battery will be on a flank, as ordered, at a
" distance equal to the depth of the strongest column in rear
" of the alignment, unless they are formed for inspection, or
" review, in which case they will be dressed with the leaders'
" heads on the alignment. In echellon the battery will be
" on a flank.

" When squares are formed in echellon, and the battery
" is brought into action, the muzzles of the guns should be
" in line with the rear base of the rear square.

" N.B.—A battery on all occasions to keep its full inter-
" val when possible.

" It is the duty of the commander of the artillery to
" keep his battery so well in hand that he may never inter-
" fere with deployments, or other movements of the brigade;
" and the brigadier should impress upon the officers com-
" manding regiments, that they should at all times give way
" to the guns when the latter have occasion to advance or re-
" tire through the line, by smartly wheeling back a section
" or company.

" Should skirmishers be in front of the battery and be
" obliged to retire, they should only retire to the guns, and
" remain with them as long as they continue in action, re-
" tiring with them.

" Should the battery be detached from the brigade, two
" companies at least should accompany it as an escort.

" These remarks apply equally to horse artillery when
" working with cavalry."

Section 2. *Review of Two or more Battalions.* (*p.* 506.)

" When two or more battalions are inspected together,
" they will either be formed in line with intervals of six

" paces between them, and proceed in the same manner as a
" single battalion, observing the additional directions that are
" given with respect to regiments in brigade, or be formed,
" should the reviewing general think proper, in a line of
" columns.

" In this section the commands are printed as in Part VI.

" 1. *Formation in Columns.*—The troops will be formed
" in a line of contiguous battalion columns at quarter distance.

OFFICERS AND COLOURS WILL TAKE POST IN REVIEW ORDER.
Officers and Colours to the Front.
Quick-March.

{ " 2. On the word *Front*, from their com-
" manders, the officers of each battalion will
" recover their swords, and on the word *March*
" they will move up to the front, and place
" themselves two paces in front of the column,
" the colours being in the centre, and the officers
" sized from flanks to centre, and at equal dis-
" tances from each other, the adjutant on their
" left.

" 3. The commanding officer will be three paces in front
" of the colours, the remaining field officers two paces in
" front of the line of officers, dividing the distances between
" the commanding officer and the flanks; the paymaster,
" surgeons, and quartermaster will be in rear of the batta-
" lion, the staff serjeants in rear of them.

" 4. The general officer commanding will be stationed in
" front of the centre of the line, the generals of divisions in
" front of the centre of their divisions, and the brigadiers in
" front of the centre of their brigade; their distances from
" the line will depend on the strength of the body of troops,
" and will be determined by the general commanding.

" 5. The band and drums will move up and form in
" several ranks on the right of battalions, their front being in
" line with the leading company.

" 6. The pioneers will be in two ranks in rear of the
" drums.

" 7. The reviewing general will be saluted without open-
" ing ranks, the men presenting arms, the officers saluting,
" the colours flying or being lowered, according to regulation,
" and the bands playing. After the salute the troops will
" be ordered to shoulder arms, and the general will go down
" the line.

<small>OFFICERS AND COLOURS WILL TAKE POST WITH THEIR BATTALIONS. *Officers and Colours take Post. Quick–March.*</small>
" 8. On the command, *Officers and Colours
" take Post*, the officers of each battalion will
" face outwards from the centre, the ensigns
" carrying the colours facing to the left; and on
" the words *Quick—March*, the whole will move
" back to their places in column, the bands,
" drums, and pioneers taking post in rear.

" 9. When the bands of a brigade have been practised
" together, they should form as one band thirty paces in rear
" of the centre of the line, the pioneers of the brigade ten
" paces in their front, and before marching past, they should
" both move to the head of the leading column.

" 10. When troops are drawn up in line for inspection
" or review, after the salute has been paid to the reviewing
" officer, the generals of divisions, brigadiers, and officers
" commanding battalions, will post themselves upon that flank
" of their divisions, brigades, or battalions to which he re-
" pairs, where they will receive him and will accompany him
" to the extent of their respective commands, after which they
" will resume their original posts.

" When troops are reviewed in line of contiguous columns,
" the generals of divisions and the brigadiers only will ac-
" company the reviewing general to the extent of their re-
" spective commands, the commanding officers of battalions
" remaining at their posts."

" 1. *Marching past in Columns.*—Points will be placed
" by a staff officer in the same manner as they are placed for
" a single battalion.

TAKE GROUND TO THE RIGHT IN FOURS. *Form Fours–Right. Quick–March.*
" 2. On the caution from the general, TAKE
" GROUND TO THE RIGHT IN FOURS, the com-
" manders will order their battalions to form
" fours to the right, and on his signal they
" will give the words *Quick—March.*

" 3. Each battalion in succession, when it has cleared
" the first point, will receive the words *Front—Turn*, from
" its commander, and at every succeeding angle will wheel to
" the left in double time, receiving the words *Forward—*
" *Quick* when square, an interval of twenty-five paces being
" preserved between the columns. It may sometimes be
" necessary to continue at the double for a short distance
" after the word *Forward*, to prevent crowding or to correct
" distances. The officers should be ordered to change their
" flanks before commencing the wheel which brings them into
" the saluting base, and will return to their former places
" after the following wheel, on the words *Forward—Quick by*
" *the Left.*

" 4. The battalion having wheeled into the saluting
" base, and taken up the quick time, will come to the shoulder
" by word of command. Each column, when it has passed
" the general, will be ordered to slope arms. Troops armed
" with the short rifle will march past in quarter-distance
" column, with trailed arms.

" 5. When marching past in quarter-distance column,
" the mounted officers only will salute ; and each general of
" a division, or the brigadier, if a single brigade is being
" reviewed, will move out after he has saluted and place him-
" self near the reviewing general whilst his column is passing.

" 6. After marching past, the leading column will be
" halted on the original alignment, and the remaining columns

" will close upon it to six paces' interval; the general will
" then order the mass to wheel into line of columns, and pro-
" ceed with his intended movements; or the columns may be
" wheeled into line in succession as they arrive at their places
" in the alignment."

" *Marching past in Open Column.*—After each column
" has wheeled into the saluting base, in quarter distance,
" it may be halted and ordered to open from the front and
" march past in open column."

" *Marching past in ' Grand Divisions.'*—Battalions may
" march past in columns of double companies, which will be
" called ' Grand Divisions ;' they will be formed as follows :
" the left companies will move up on the left of the right
" companies, that is, No. 2 on the left of No. 1, No. 4 on the
" left of No. 3, and so on, the captains will be posted on the
" outward flanks of their companies; the grand divisions will
" march past by the right at company distance from each
" other. This is an exceptional formation, only to be used
" in marching past; the ordinary column will be re-formed
" before the manœuvres commence."

" *Advancing in Review Order.*—At the end of the review,
" if required to do so by the reviewing general, the columns
" will be formed on their original ground in review order, the
" officers and colours in front, as described in the first part of
" this section; they will then advance in slow time, the bands
" and drums playing, and when at a convenient distance from
" the reviewing general, which must vary according to the
" extent of the line, they will be halted and ordered to salute
" as described in paragraph 7 of the first part of this section,
" after which they will be ordered to shoulder arms and will
" proceed as directed by the general."

"The following is the Order of March to be
"observed at Reviews performed before the
"Sovereign; and is also to be observed, in as
"far as it is applicable, at all Reviews before
"General Officers.

"1. Detachment of life guards, or other cavalry, pre-
"ceded by an officer of the quarter-master-general's depart-
"ment.
"2. The Sovereign's led horses.
"3. Aides-de-camp to the commander-in-chief.
"4. Aides-de-camp to the Sovereign.
"5. Deputy adjutant-general, deputy quarter-master-
"general, and equerries in waiting to the Sovereign.
"6. Adjutant-general, military secretary to the com-
"mander-in-chief, quarter-master-general.
"7. Commander-in-chief.
"8. Princes of the blood.
"9. The Sovereign.
"10. Gold stick in waiting, and master of the horse, if
"present.
"11. Foreign general officers, general officers and colonels
"on the staff in successive order, according to rank and seni-
"ority, followed by such other general officers, not upon the
"staff, as may be present, and equerries and attendants upon
"the foreign princes.
"12. Assistant adjutant-general, assistant quarter-mas-
"ter-general, and deputy assistants.
"13. Aides-de-camp and majors of brigade to general
"officers on the staff.
"14. Royal carriages.
"15. Detachments of cavalry."

[*The following Memorandum was sent from the Horse Guards for*
WORDS OF COMMAND

After the Cautionary Words of Command from the Division General have been repeated by the Brigadiers and Commanders of Battalions, and the Battalion Cautions have been given by the latter, one G will be sounded on a trumpet or bugle, on hearing which the Commanders of Battalions will give their final executive words.

Words of Command that are given only by the Brigadier will be repeated

Division Generals' Commands.	Brigadiers' Commands.	Commanders of Battalions' Commands.	Captains' Commands.
	Officers will take post in Review Order.	Officers will take post in Review Order. Officers to the Front, Quick March.	
General Salute.	General Salute.	General Salute. (*Signal.*) Present—Arms.	
The Division will Shoulder.	The Brigade will Shoulder.	The Brigade will Shoulder. (*Signal.*) Shoulder—Arms.	
	Officers will take post with their Battalions.	Officers will take post with their Battalions. Officers take post. (*Signal.*) Quick—March.	
	The Brigade will take ground to the right in fours.	The Brigade will take ground to the right in fours. Battalion, Fours—Right. (*Signal.*) Quick—March. Front—Turn. Officers commanding Companies, change your flanks. Left Wheel—Double. Forward. Quick. By the Right. Halt—Dress.	
	The Brigade will march past in Open Column.	The Brigade will march past in open Column. Shoulder—Arms. Advance by successive Companies from the front at Wheeling distance. Leading Company, Quick—March.	No. 2. Quick —March. No. 3. Quick —March, &c.

adoption at a large Review of Volunteers, held at Gloucester, in 1860.]

FOR A REVIEW.

by the Commanders of Battalions; this done, the Brigadier will hold up his sword as a signal, on which the Commanders of Battalions will give their executive words.

The word (*Signal*) is introduced in the column of commands for Commanders of Battalions, to show what portion of their commands are given before the Signal, and what portion after it.

Division Generals' Commands.	Brigadiers' Commands.	Commanders of Battalions' Commands.	Captains' Commands.
		On the March close to Quarter distance on the leading Company, remaining Companies—Double.	No. 2. Quick. No. 3. Quick. &c., &c.
		Battalion, Left Wheel—Double. Forward—Quick, By the Left.	
		Battalion, Left Wheel—Double. Forward—Quick.	
		Battalion, Left Wheel—Double. Halt, Dress.	
	Officers will take post in Review Order.	Officers will take post in Review Order. Officers to the Front. (*Signal.*) Quick—March.	
The Division will advance in Review Order, in Quick Time.	The Brigade will advance in Review Order, in Quick Time.	The Brigade will advance in Review Order, in Quick Time. Battalion will advance. (*Signal.*) Quick—March.	
The Division will Halt.	The Brigade will Halt.	The Brigade will Halt. (*Signal.*) Battalion—Halt.	
General Salute.	General Salute.	General Salute. (*Signal.*) Present—Arms.	
The Division will Shoulder.	The Brigade will Shoulder.	The Battalion will Shoulder. (*Signal.*) Shoulder—Arms.	
Officers will take post with their Battalion.	Officers will take post with their Battalion.	(*Signal.*) Officers will take post with their Battalions. Officers take post, Quick—March.	
The Division will Order and Stand at Ease.	The Brigade will Order and Stand at Ease.	The Brigade will Order and Stand at Ease. Order Arms—Stand at Ease.	

D. LYSONS, *Colonel*, **A.A.G.**

THE FOLLOWING COPY OF AN ORDER IS INSERTED, AS IN AN ENCLOSED COUNTY LIKE DEVONSHIRE, IT MAY BE FOUND OF ADVANTAGE TO PRACTISE THE DEFENSIVE PLAN OF RETIRING THEREIN ENJOINED.

Devonport, 15*th February*, 1862.

DISTRICT ORDER.

With respect to out-post duties in this neighbourhood, as it is not laid down in the *Field Exercise* how picquets driven in by an enemy are to retire in an enclosed country, the major-general requests that the following instructions may be followed:—

1. The supposed object is to retard the advance of the enemy until our troops, covered by the picquets, can take up some strong defensive position.

2. The enemy will be retarded if he be exposed from time to time, while pursuing by the roads, to a destructive fire which he cannot return with much injury to us. He is equally retarded if, in consequence of his losses, he is compelled to quit the roads and traverse the adjacent fields, cutting a way through the hedges and banks.

3. To make this vigorous opposition, it is obvious that the picquets must not retire as in skirmishing order across a plain. One picquet, say of the ordinary strength of a company, is quite sufficient to cover any body of troops retiring through the Devonshire lanes; but its commander must know how to handle it properly.

4. He will collect his men in one body. While retiring in fours, he will watch every turn of the road. At such spots it will generally be found that there is a bank behind which a few men could shelter themselves, and in safety enfilade an advancing party. *There* a few of the leading files will be placed, in order to fire upon the supposed pursuing enemy.

5. Good cover of any kind, walls, trees, &c., will be taken advantage of in a similar manner. Frequently banks extending up hill and at right angles to the road present themselves, which would serve as a parapet to the defenders, and enfilade a considerable length of the road; but judgment is required to resist the temptation of placing men in positions from which, although they could in safety greatly annoy the enemy, they would not be able to retire without unduly exposing themselves.

6. When compelled to retire they will do so in double time, concealing themselves as much as possible, and rejoin the rear of the picquet.

7. It must be expected, notwithstanding the delay it would occasion him, that the enemy will send out skirmishers to take the firing parties in flank. These skirmishers will be more or less opposed by fresh skirmishers; in such case the picquet would be strengthened from the main body. In skirmishing over an enclosed country like Devonshire, the defence has great advantage over the attack.

8. The more obstinately the picquets dispute the ground by a succession of well selected posts,

the more time is afforded to the main body and guns falling back, to take up a previously determined position.

9. On nearing this position, the picquet will run in quickly, that it may not mask the fire of the defenders.

10. Were an enemy to effect a landing in force at Torbay, it is in this manner that his advance towards Plymouth would be resisted.

Devonport, 25th February, 1862.

DISTRICT ORDER*.

1. In the revised edition of the *Field Exercise* just issued, it is repeated (p. 218) that when a battalion is drilled singly, it should move as a component part of a brigade, and make changes of position and formations, on points dressed on previously determined alignments.

2. No commanding officer can do his regiment justice on brigade field days, unless, on all occasions of battalion drill under himself, the adjutant, or others, he insists upon that order being carried out.

3. Previous to all movements in double or single column, and to all advances or retirements in direct echellon, a caution should be given, stating that his battalion moves either as the directing battalion, or regulated by a supposed battalion on

---

* The Order referred to in note, p. 19.

its right or left. Occasionally he will place a point to mark the nearest flank of the supposed adjacent battalion from which he may have to preserve distance.

4. When his is the supposed directing battalion, he will invariably furnish the mounted point (or points) from which the supposed adjacent battalion (or battalions) may have to take distance, &c.

5. The advances and retirements in column should nearly always be made as if the supposed brigade were formed of battalions at deploying distance.

6. It is not clearly laid down in Section 16, p. 261, that columns are to be practised in wheels of less than a quarter circle; but Section 5, p. 464, shows that they should be so practised. At battalion drill it will be found of advantage to halt wheeling quarter distance (or close) columns at very uncertain periods,—occasionally allowing them to wheel the entire circle.

7. In all deployments and formation of lines, a distant point should be previously determined on. In a barrack square, the corner of a building, or a lamp-post, &c., will serve the purpose in a more unswerving and honest manner, than most mounted or unmounted points.

8. The major-general expects that this plan will be adopted in all battalion movements, and he hopes to be able to report at his next half yearly inspection, that they are executed in a satisfactory manner.

FINIS.

www.ingramcontent.com/pod-product-compliance
Lightning Source LLC
Chambersburg PA
CBHW030320170426
43202CB00009B/1078